# THE RIGHT SIDE
## OF THE
# EQUATION

# THE RIGHT SIDE OF THE EQUATION

## MASTERING RELATIONAL INTELLIGENCE

# JUD BOIES

Thrive Publications
Granite Bay, California

THE RIGHT SIDE OF THE EQUATION

Published by Thrive Publications
PO Box 2336
Granite Bay, CA 95746

Design: Tim Chambers

First printing, 2006

Printed in the United States of America

ISBN 0-9779306-1-0

*This book would not exist without the input and experiences of the people and companies who have deployed the* RIGHT SIDE OF THE EQUATION. *It also would not exist without the contributions of Dr. Gil Stieglitz, Gary Basham, Cathy Hamilton, Kevin Robertson and Vicki Newman. Thank you to my wife, Mary, and my daughters, Paige and Kelly, for your patience, support and for allowing me to live out the* RIGHT SIDE OF THE EQUATION *in my own life.*

# Contents

# 1

# Relational Intelligence

AT SOME POINT IN TIME everyone becomes relationally unconscious. We become relationally absent, oblivious to the feelings and needs of other people. It's not meant to be malicious; we just get distracted. Life gets busy, so we revert to task mode. Sometimes relationships get hard, or stale. It seems easier to let it go, so we do. But being relationally unconscious is like falling asleep at the wheel; and people are the driving forces of our lives.

Conversely, Relational Intelligence is an awakening to the needs of others and responding. It is becoming learned in the art of relationship—not to manipulate, but to genuinely care. Relational Intelligence takes the blinders off so you can truly see the people you are working or living with. It is then that you will begin to see changes. The people in the workplace become more cooperative. Your home life experiences harmony. Your marriage thrives, and your children's attitudes change for the better. Master Relational Intelligence and you will experience levels of success you never knew existed.

The key to Relational Intelligence is making sure we understand what the people around us need in order for us to meet our goals. If you seek to pursue, please and meet the needs of the people around you, they will respond positively, reaching solutions that will lead to met goals. Your personal and professional needs will be taken care of in the process, with a lot less hassle.

There is an equation for understanding and accomplishing our needs, goals and objectives. Half of the equation is determining what you want. This is the left side of the equation. The other half is determining what it will take from a people point of view to accomplish those goals and objectives. This is the *Right Side of the Equation*. On average, we spend more than 90% of our time and attention on the left side. When we devote only 10% or less to the *Right Side of the Equation* we become relationally unconscious. We wonder why we aren't successful at what we're trying to accomplish. We've invested time and energy executing the plan through tasks, but we haven't invested in the people side of the equation. Why is this?

I believe it's because we don't know how. We're out of practice. We've forgotten how to pursue loved ones, genuinely please others, and therefore have no idea how to actually meet their needs. The *Right Side of the Equation* is a straightforward approach that takes away any guesswork. When you learn to balance the left and the right sides, it will become easier to reach your goals.

We must focus on the *Right Side of the Equation* because we are relational beings. We need people around us. It's one of the top two or three most important things in our lives. Let me prove it to you. I've asked several thousand people to name the most important things in their lives with this question: "If you were on an island with sufficient food, water, and shelter, but could choose three additional things, what would you choose? Or say you chose to go on a mission to another planet for several years? Or what if you were the last living person on earth? What three things would you want to take that would be appropriate in all three situations? Take a moment and write them down:

1  _____

2  _____

3  _____

Every time I ask this question, I get the same three answers. One of the top three is people (you'll read about the other two later on). In every scenario, we want loved ones with us. Why? Because we are relational—no man is an island. From the moment we are born, we need people.

During the first 16–18 years of life we experience a balance between relationships and accomplishing goals. The first five years are entirely spent with other people—parents, caregivers, and friends. Then in elementary school, we learn to balance schoolwork, chores, and spending time with our friends and family.

But then the shift begins. Sometime around junior high, we start to put acquisition and achievement (the left side of the equation) ahead of relationships and personal needs (the *Right Side of the Equation*). Our quest for more becomes insatiable and takes hold at the expense of the right side. We become so interested in what we want to achieve, we forget the people around us. We become relationally unconscious. We forget that we need people to accomplish anything. Try being married by yourself. Try being a parent when you're never home. Try selling a product without loyal customers. Try building a business without employees. It doesn't work.

There is a solution and it works. You'll enjoy applying this solution because you will have your own needs met while helping those around you meet their needs. But first, a disclaimer.

This is not a touchy-feely book. The program explained is not a touchy-feely program. It's designed for everyone who has become relationally unconscious who would like to become relationally intelligent. It focuses on key factors of relationships such as the character, competency, chemistry, capability and contribution necessary to make things work.

You will learn the *Right Side of the Equation* through the story of Todd Hanson. He was somewhat successful, but was tossed about by whatever life handed him. He had no concept of Relational Intelligence. But then his life shifts when he goes to work for Blake Severson, a business owner who mastered Relational Intelligence through the *Right Side of the Equation* program. If you don't want to read about Todd's life, skip to Chapter Six, where Todd begins to learn the fundamentals of the program. Though Todd is a fictional character, every experience he has is real. I have witnessed the life of Todd Hanson through my friends, customers, business associates and myself.

The program is real. It has been taught to thousands of employees and people over the past ten years. By implementing these principles, you can learn to master Relational Intelligence— through the *Right Side of the Equation.*

## CHAPTER SUMMARY

- At some point, everyone becomes relationally unconscious.

- If something is failing in your life, check to see if it's because you've been relationally unconscious.

- To be successful, you must become relationally intelligent.

- The key to Relational Intelligence is the *Right Side of the Equation*.

- The *Right Side of the Equation* is understanding how to pursue, please and meet the needs of the people around you so they will help you reach your goals.

- The left side of the equation is our goal for acquisition and achievement.

- This book provides a simple three-step process for balancing the *Right Side of the Equation* with the left side of the equation.

**POINTS TO PONDER**

- Are you more focused on the goals in your life than on the people it will take to accomplish those goals?

- Is there an area of your life that's failing?

  — Is it because you've failed in the relationships in that area?

- Are you relationally unconscious?

# Growing Up in America

"YOUR FATHER LEFT US."

Todd Hanson could think of nothing else. Earlier, he had come home to Mom waiting on the couch, tissue in hand. She blurted it out as soon as he walked in the door, and in an instant, his 12-year-old life changed. On the outside, he stood motionless. On the inside, he felt a blow to the gut. It was a blur from then on—another woman—an apartment on the other side of town—divorce papers signed. At first, shock numbed him, but then anger set in.

He didn't understand. They had a great family: his brother Mark and their sister, Penny. The Hansons lived in the suburbs, the kind of neighborhood where the kids played in the yards while parents visited. Dad worked at a local tile plant as a shift supervisor, and Mom was a teacher. They made enough money to live comfortably, never experiencing real need. They had new clothes at the beginning of each school year and got what they wanted for Christmas and birthdays. Every summer they took a family vacation. They spent many nights laughing together at the dinner table. It seemed like life couldn't get much better.

Up until then, life had been relatively simple for Todd. He'd known Grant, Cole, and Brian for as long as he could remember. There were few memories that didn't include at least one of them. Catching frogs down at the river. Taking swim lessons at the YMCA. Enduring Mrs. Parker's pop math quizzes in fourth grade. Camping trips, barbecues, and raking leaves in the fall. They even had a secret handshake.

During those years, they'd dream together. What do we want to be when we grow up? At one point, Cole decided he would be an astronaut. Brian thought he'd be a fireman. Todd wanted to be on television. Grant just wanted a Corvette. Even when life got complicated with parents or sisters, they were there for each other. There was nothing a close go-cart race or an afternoon fishing trip couldn't handle. Todd now yearned for the simplicity of those years.

Divorce wasn't something new. Of the three friends he grew up with, two of them were in single parent homes. His best friend, Grant, lived next door with his mom. His bedroom window was fifteen feet from Todd's, and the two often left their windows open in the summer, talking instead of sleeping. Grant's folks had divorced when he was eight, and, though Grant never knew it, Todd sometimes heard him crying for his dad in his sleep. He now shuddered at the thought.

After his parents' divorce, life got complicated. There were no more happy times around the dinner table. Family vacations disappeared. When he spent time with his dad, the girlfriend was there. To make things worse, Todd listened to his mom bad-mouth his dad night after night. Todd didn't disagree with her, but it was like picking the scab off a wound over and over.

His grades dropped. He hated his parents. And it came at a time when he felt vulnerable to the opinions of his classmates. The fact that half the kids in his school had divorced parents didn't make him feel any better.

## THINK IT THROUGH

*Was your childhood similar to Todd's? Did your parents talk to you about what was most important in life? How were your goals and dreams established? You may not have known there could be goals for your family, friends, school, etc. For example, your parents could have made goals such as, "We're going to stay married this year and build a growing and thriving marriage in which we are both happy," a left side of the equation goal. It could have been followed by a Right Side of the Equation goal describing what they had to do for each other to accomplish this goal.*

*How do you think your childhood shaped who you are today? Are many of your beliefs, values, and current goals still based on some of the earliest memories of your childhood? You enjoyed spending a lot of time in relationship with your friends, classmates and family. Has that shifted?*

*If you are like most people, life just passed by. You may have been taught what was right and wrong. Perhaps you were taught that it was okay to want things and that possessions bring happiness. But did the thought ever cross your mind how people played into getting the things you wanted? It may have been a given that you didn't need to think about people because it was so obvious.*

*What do you think was the impact of the divorce between Todd's parents in other areas of their life? No doubt it had an impact on their capability at work. They may have been competent to complete the goals of their jobs, but I suspect they were incapable of doing that job for many days while they were in the midst of the divorce. Studies show the average employee is 25% less productive for the 12-month period surrounding a divorce.*

*The crisis in Todd's life could've been avoided
with a plan focused on what was important.*

### JUNIOR HIGH AND HIGH SCHOOL—THE SHIFT BEGINS

In junior high, Todd began to notice there was a "status" and "pecking order" based on perceptions of where people stood relating to their acquisitions and achievements. It was the clothes you wore, whether you played sports, and whom you hung out with that shaped your identity. His awareness of the pecking order became prominent in a subconscious way. The left side of the equation was becoming the primary standard for measurement of a person, not on who they were.

Todd muddled his way through junior high coping with the pain and baggage of his parents' divorce. His freshman year in high school wasn't much better. His pain subsided gradually through the focus on other endeavors, such as football games, girls, and classes. He drifted through the year, rolling with the punches, looking forward to the next new thing. But then in his sophomore year, Todd met someone who would have an impact. It was his auto shop teacher, Mr. Brooks. Mr. Brooks was the first person Todd met who had some understanding of Relational Intelligence.

"Okay, men, break into groups of four and choose a leader. You have two minutes. Go!" The sound of shuffling chairs and chatter filled the room. Mr. Brooks pushed his glasses back, rearranged some items on his makeshift desk, and glanced about the class. Todd moved closer to Grant, Brian and Cole, and then agreed he would lead. The noise died down a bit, and Mr. Brooks resumed instruction.

"Auto shop is more than changing spark plugs," he began. "We will rebuild a car to compete against my other classes. These cars are auctioned off at the end of the year and we donate the proceeds to programs that need the money. Your team of four will be assigned what part of the car you will work on. It will require planning, discipline, and teamwork. If you stick with it, your class could bring in the most money. This is a much sought-after privilege, so the competition will be fierce. There is one catch, though. You must have passing grades in your other courses to stay in my class. This is non-negotiable!"

Todd felt himself getting excited. He and his buddies were assigned the interior of the car. They didn't know a thing about upholstery, headliners, and gauges, but Mr. Brooks could teach them that. One thing Todd did know— his class was going to win this competition.

Mr. Brooks taught them about more than rebuilding a car. He turned his lessons into a logical system for approaching any problem. He had a specific game plan laid out in a logical format that fit on a page. His students saw the program, its goals, and the plan to carry it through. He broke the complex operation into segments and put a team in charge of each section. So their work would integrate smoothly with that of the other teams, Mr. Brooks provided a formula for organizing their time and setting the goals needed to meet deadlines.

The sophomore year ended quite successfully for Todd and his friends. Their car interior took first place among all the auto shop classes, and their car brought in the most money. They had the prestige of winning the competition, and received an award for their efforts.

In the meantime, Todd and his pals caught the car bug. Todd's parents bought him his first car, and he set about using what he had learned in auto shop to customize it, making it better and faster.

Mr. Brooks continued to be a major influence through high school. He made Todd and Brian his assistants, training them on the latest technology and providing access to the correct tools. He then worked out employment for Todd at a local car dealership—his first job. Along with Todd's parents, he encouraged him to go to college. By graduation, Todd was accepted by a local college, but decided on a school 150 miles away. Mr. Brooks felt it was the best suited to Todd's interests.

## THINK IT THROUGH

*Mr. Brooks understood Relational Intelligence. He spent an extraordinary amount of time with Todd on the Right Side of the Equation. He talked to him about success in his life, man to man, even though he was in a position of authority as his teacher. He showed that he cared about Todd and was a positive impact in his life.*

*Do you think this was rewarding to Mr. Brooks? Yes, and you will experience some of the same rewards when you deploy the Right Side of the Equation in the lives of the people around you. But it needs to be deliberate. You must know you are working on the Right Side of the Equation and not just let it happen. We are intentional about our left side goals, but now it's time to be intentional about our right side actions.*

## AN OPPOSING INFLUENCE SETS IN

Going with the flow of high school, Todd lived life day to day. His latest attention-grabber was an exciting new social scene. Todd's girlfriend was popular, so they were invited to weekend parties at the "in crowd" houses. Todd arranged for his three buddies to come along. This was a big boost for his ego. They hung out with people who had a completely different lifestyle. The biggest difference was the instant availability of drugs and alcohol. The parents of these young people, many divorced, had decided that all kids were sure to indulge, so they might as well do it at home. It would keep them off the streets, they reasoned. It didn't occur to them that everyone visiting the party had to drive there. These parties were huge and involved more than just beer. The kids gained favor by showing up with a bottle of vodka or a couple of joints. As inhibitions faded, hormones surged. It wasn't really a party unless you had a few too many drinks and tried to go as far as possible with your girlfriend—or any available girl. Besides cars and their futures, Todd and his buddies now talked about how cool last weekend's party was, how plowed they were and how far things got with their girlfriends.

## THINK IT THROUGH

*Recognize the shift here. These parties were about what they could acquire in the way of drugs and alcohol, who you were seen with (as a boost for the ego), and what they could accomplish in terms of alcohol consumption or achievement with their girlfriends. It wasn't as much about relationships as it was about achieving. Slowly but surely the left side of the equation took hold and relational unconsciousness crept in.*

*But as you will see, the left side alone is empty or, at best, far less fulfilling than the combination of both the left and the right sides.*

## THE FATEFUL NIGHT

Todd sat in the back seat of Grant's car, his thoughts racing.

It was a Friday night like many others. Someone's parents were away for the weekend, so that's where the party was held. They had a full bar and marijuana going, then someone brought in cocaine. It had been crazy—people drinking, dancing, and the girls especially affectionate. He'd had a blast.

Cole had gone to the party alone and finally hooked up with Sherry, a girl he'd had his eyes on all year. They seemed to really hit it off, and then they left together. That was the last he'd seen of Cole.

Rita, Cole's mother, called him about 3:30 in the morning. Cole had been hurt in a car accident. They suspected a drunk driver crossed over into his lane. Todd called Brian and Grant, and the three were on their way to the hospital.

At the hospital, Cole's mother met them in the waiting room. "Todd, where were you guys tonight?" she demanded.

"Uh, just a party at a friend's."

"Was Cole drinking?"

"I-I don't think so." He looked at his friends, unsure of what he should say. Grant and Brian just stood there.

Just then, a doctor, nurse, and chaplain from the hospital appeared. They led Rita to a chair and told her that Cole had died from massive internal bleeding. Sherry was killed instantly. Though it was little comfort, the doctor said Cole's blood alcohol level was only .02. He probably had less than one 12-ounce beer.

For Todd, the pain of his folks divorcing was insignificant compared to this. How could this happen? They drove away from the hospital in the eerie predawn light, numb with shock. He wanted to cry, but held it in. He wanted to talk, but didn't know what to say. He wanted answers, but didn't know what questions to ask. He didn't want to go home. He didn't want to be alone, but he didn't want to be with Brian and Grant, either.

The only thing he was sure about was the pain.

In the end, they bought some donuts and went to the river—a place they went to sort things out. How could Cole and Sherry be gone? This wasn't supposed to happen to teenagers.

The boys spent four hours sulking. They then realized they had to face their parents and the inevitable barrage of questions about the previous evening.

By the time he arrived home, Todd's mother had learned the details of what had happened. A college student who had been drinking at a fraternity party hit Cole's car. She was in pretty good condition with a broken arm and leg, plus some cuts and scrapes. But her life was about to change as she faced the consequences of killing two people.

Todd was surprised that neither his mother nor father ever asked the tough questions. Both were glad he was safe and figured that, because it was someone else's fault, Todd and his friends had simply been enjoying a normal evening. To them, Cole and Sherry were victims of a tragic situation.

Todd knew differently, as did most of the people at the party. Any one of them could have caused the accident. Any one of them could've been sentenced to prison.

Eventually Todd, Grant, and Brian returned to the parties. They had persuaded themselves that a freak accident had happened to someone else. It couldn't possibly happen to them.

At graduation, there was a moment of silence for the two dead students. Todd wished Cole were there with him when he later celebrated—at a party with drugs and alcohol.

## THINK IT THROUGH

*This tragedy is not uncommon. Though this exact event may not have taken place in your immediate family or with a co-worker, we will experience painful situations in our lives. How will you and the people around you respond to it? Todd, Grant and Brian had each other to spend time with and work through the pain and misery that followed. In their case, it would be something they would never forget.*

*But how would the co-workers of Cole's parents respond to them? How would they help them through their pain, misery and certain drop in job performance? The changes may be so severe that they might lose their jobs. Wouldn't that add insult to the pain?*

*Todd was experiencing many realities of our society. He worked and made money. He thought he should acquire and achieve. He made decisions based on what he thought others expected of him. He had gone through a family divorce. And he experienced the pain of death.*

*With all those events, he still had had no discussions about the most meaningful things in life. He still did not know how to live his life intentionally, focusing on meaningful priorities. Life carried Todd forward.*

*Are your high school memories similar? Did your experiences help shape your character? Who Todd became was established between birth and the end of high school, yet it all happened by chance. Nobody told Todd he could shape his future and build lifelong goals while learning history and science. He didn't learn that there were important things in life that could bring fulfillment and happiness if he built his life around them. He wasn't told there was a strategy to success. Most importantly, he had no concept of Relational Intelligence or about being intentional about the Right Side of the Equation.*

*No deliberate plan for success.*

### LIFE BEGINS AFTER HIGH SCHOOL

Todd allowed the summer after graduation to simply pass by. He partied most weekends. He worked at the dealership during the week. He hung out with his girlfriend or the guys in the evenings. Life may have resembled some balance between the right and the left, but it was purely by accident. There was no plan, no objective and no conscious awareness to what he should be working on relating to the equation. He was in limbo between true relational unconsciousness and relational awareness.

Then at the end of summer, Todd broke up with his girlfriend, said goodbye to his buddies, and moved into the dorms at college. His first objective was to find a group of people he enjoyed being with. It was a *Right Side of the Equation* need he had to fill. He found it in the fraternity system.

"Up and at it, Maggot! I need breakfast!"

Todd's body responded, but his mind took a few seconds to catch up. "Oh, yeah, rush week," he thought. "I'm pledging for Sigma Alpha Sigma."

It was an exhausting initiation process, but he did it. They accepted him. And it was worth it.

Todd liked fraternity life. It meant instant friends that closely resembled the group he was part of back in high school. It was a brotherhood (at least that's what they called it) that went beyond college. It met a deep need he had for relationships. Todd appreciated that Sigma Alpha Sigma valued academics, relationships with others, and high standards for how to behave as a man. These things were emphasized every day.

Though partying was hearty on weekends, everyone studied during the week. This was a first for Todd. He had never taken academics seriously in high school, but now it felt like the right thing to do.

By the end of his freshman year, Todd had a 3.12 grade-point average. He had become active in the fraternity leadership and took the post of "Fraternity Philanthropy," responsible for leading community projects. And he had met a girl at one of the sorority/fraternity parties.

The next two years were a time of rapid maturing for Todd. He found a good balance between studying, partying on weekends with his fraternity brothers, and dating. He dated several girls and enjoyed the variety. He never experienced the same "puppy love" he had had with his high school girlfriend. Even then he had known she wasn't going to be his life-long love. Hanging out with the guys was Todd's first choice. Dating was more of a necessity, allowing him to be with a girl from time to time.

However, the fraternity wasn't the best influence on how to treat women. When the guys got together, a group mentality took over. They focused more on conquests than the qualities of the girl. There was no such thing as a "relationship." It was more like "date them and rate them." For Todd, the fraternity came first. Hanging out with the guys was priority one. The talk was the same as it had been in high school: the jobs they'd have, the places they'd live, the families they'd raise, and how they'd never make the same mistakes as their parents.

Between their junior and senior years, Brian got married. Todd and Grant helped Brian find a place to live and plan the honeymoon. Brian had saved enough for a down payment on a small house with just enough left over for a weeklong trip to Hawaii. During their time together, they spent a lot of time reminiscing about their childhoods. They remembered their conversations about what they would be when they grew up. Now, they were growing up, and Brian was taking a first step into manhood. They also reflected on Cole and how he didn't get his future.

During his senior year, Todd realized he had accomplished a lot. He had completed three years of college, worked summers to earn money to help with his schooling, and became president of Sigma Alpha Sigma. He had more than a hundred close friends he now considered brothers—well, fraternity brothers—which was every bit as good as blood brothers in his mind.

As the year progressed, Todd interviewed with some of the many companies recruiting at his school. Many alumni called him to interview with their companies. He had seen many of his older fraternity brothers and friends go through this process in previous years and land great jobs, the first step to their job-home-family dreams.

Todd's senior year was a positive time in his life. As fraternity president, he had achieved real status. Many looked to him as a leader. He set the tone for the house and was well-counseled by the alumni who had been there before him. Much of what Mr. Brooks taught him about organizing teams to accomplish projects proved very effective. He built teams within the house to manage activities like cooking and cleaning. He organized a study committee that made sure everyone maintained their grades, a fundraising committee to oversee help for those in need, and a membership-building committee. In the past, individuals had handled these activities. Todd put a minimum of two people in charge, with one spokesperson for each committee. This proved very effective. Todd's ideas attracted a lot of attention from many of the alumni, young and old. He was experiencing a glimpse of success by implementing some of what Mr. Brooks had taught him, but it was being done at the subconscious level. It wasn't part of a deliberate plan. He had little knowledge about how to lead deliberately. But it was coming.

## PERFECTION IS JUST AROUND THE CORNER

Todd had a clear picture of finishing school, marrying a nice girl, taking a great job, buying a house and raising a family. His adult life would be perfect, very different from the lives of his parents.

As it turned out, he did meet someone during his senior year that he knew was perfect. Her name was Sarah, and she came from a very stable family. Her parents were actually still married and in love with each other. She had almost the same ideas about how and where she wanted to live and what was important in life. She was also extremely attractive. She, too, was a senior and graduated with Todd.

Todd debated between offers from the two companies he liked most. Both would allow him to be based in his hometown. He liked that because he could be back with his buddies and his family. Sarah was committed to Todd and didn't really care where he worked as long as he brought her with him. He accepted a job as a regional salesman for an automobile supply company called Regent Wholesale. He preferred this job because it related to his continued love for cars. Also, he worked with all the car dealerships in the area, including his previous employer where Brian and Grant now worked. His job was to sell dealerships the consumable supplies used in their repair shops such as batteries, light bulbs, and windshield wipers.

Regent Wholesale was quite large, over 500 employees nationwide, and based in California. The job provided him with a brand new car every two years, an expense account for taking clients to lunch and sporting events and a healthy income. It wasn't the six figures he had hoped for, but if he worked hard enough, there was a commission plan that would allow him to make $100,000. He did his homework and knew more than 60% of their regional salesmen reached this goal.

Todd was now a young adult. He continued to mature, but as in school, life just happened. He followed the path established by school curriculum and then by his company. Before his graduation, his mother or father occasionally asked him what direction he wanted to take after college. This meant that Todd's life was guided by brief discussions with his folks as they tried to provide some guidance. These talks didn't discuss a plan based on values. Todd wasn't even aware that he should be thinking about such things.

## THINK IT THROUGH

*Todd's sole influence was his environment—his friends, people at his college, the company he worked for, and the media who painted a stereotypical picture of possessions and achievements. Life was a constant comparison of what he had, rated against what others had, and of what he wanted, rated against what others wanted. Though it took many years, he eventually found out that comparing acquisitions and accomplishments never leads to happiness or fulfillment.*

*Is this how your own life went? If you're still in the process, is this how your life is going? Take a look at how Todd spent the next 20 years. He was chasing the better house, better car, better vacation, acquisition of more toys and other dreams, yet none of these things ever made a difference for long. They never provided the lasting fulfillment and happiness he was looking for.*

---

### *What are you pursuing?*

---

### Chapter Summary

- We start life experiencing the balance between the left and right sides of the equation—we spend a fair amount of time developing relationships with friends and we spend a fair amount of time in school and doing chores.

- The shift in balance begins around junior high when acquisition and achievement overshadow friendships.

- Focusing on the *Right Side of the Equation* should become deliberate in junior high or high school, but seldom does.

- People don't know how to respond to tragedies—but they will through the *Right Side of the Equation*.

- We tend to let life carry us along for the ride instead of being an active participant as the driver. Has this happened to you?

- We let society influence us more toward the left side of the equation to the point that it becomes the standard topic of conversation when we do meet with our friends.

## POINTS TO PONDER

- Did you spend a fair amount of time with friends and family until you were about 18 years old?

- Did you notice a shift for acquisition and achievement sometime around junior high?

- Have you let life just carry you along?

- Do you have a plan in place that is deliberate about understanding the needs of the people around you?

# 3

# Todd Chases the Dream

WITH A GREAT JOB IN HAND, Todd and Sarah moved back to his hometown. Using her Journalism degree, she became an editorial assistant at the local newspaper. She, too, was thrilled with her job, writing articles that people read each morning.

Todd and Sarah moved into an apartment together. They talked about marriage, but neither was ready for the actual ceremony. Maybe they would get married in a year or two. Each said they were committed to the other, but wanted to settle into their jobs first.

Todd's parents were furious. At different times, both his mother and father had a conversation with him, encouraging him to make the commitment and get married. He didn't buy it. His dad had left his mom to move in with another woman, and his mom began dating shortly thereafter. What credibility did they have? Yet even though his parents were opposed to him living with Sarah, he knew somewhere deep inside that living together wasn't right.

Sarah's parents were equally disappointed. They had raised her in a home with strong moral values and had taken her to church every Sunday for as long as she could remember. They never said specifically that she mustn't live with anyone before marriage. They simply assumed she understood this was a wrong decision.

Todd's friends thought it was cool they were living together and told them so. This approval was an ego boost for both of them. Each had a great job, adequate income, and a live-in partner. It wasn't as if they needed to hold out until marriage to sleep together. That concept had long been obsolete among their friends. Sex was part of life at their age. Any initial doubt about living together was quickly overcome. Many people they knew were living together.

Todd and Sarah set up house in an apartment complex with several luxury amenities: swimming pool, tennis courts, racquetball court, rec room, game room, workout room, a lounge with a fully attended bar, nightclub, and laundry facilities. It was the kind of place where many young professionals moved. It was almost too good to be true. Like college, the complex had a social calendar. Unlike college, they didn't have to study anymore.

They found the class distinctions of junior high, high school, and college had moved up another notch. They remembered back in junior high when they had begun to categorize others by their friends, clothes, and activities. In high school, the pecking order had become stronger and more defined. In college, status hinged on where you came from or what fraternity or sorority you belonged to. Now, they had reached a new level. At every event, the topic of discussion was what job you held, what vacation you had taken, what brands you drank, and what toys you owned. Life was scored by acquisition and achievement.

What they didn't realize was that the left side of the equation makes no sense unless you have a right side to enjoy it with. Many of Todd and Sarah's new neighbors ended up in a singles' complex because they focused intently on acquisition and achievement. They became so out of balance, they lost their important relationships. They were beyond relational unconsciousness; they were in a relational coma, incapable of positive, conscious interaction with those around them. Now the best they could do was boast about their list of achievements in hopes that someone would be impressed by it and share in their success.

## SERPENT IN THE GARDEN

After six months in the complex, Todd started to notice that several single guys seemed interested in Sarah. They'd try to monopolize the conversation with Sarah or sit beside her when she was sunning herself at the pool. For the first time in Todd's life, he began to feel jealous. He was concerned whenever he had to be away for any period of time. When he asked her whether she noticed these guys were spending unusual amounts of time with her, she said she thought they were just nice guys who were lonely. His nagging concern continued.

Sarah finally learned that her "friends" were interested in more than friendship. The situation peaked when Todd was away on a business trip. One admirer ran into Sarah by the pool on a Saturday afternoon. During their conversation, she mentioned that Todd was away. After spending the afternoon talking, Sarah invited him to share some leftover spaghetti. After a few glasses of wine, he turned and kissed her. Not a thank-you kiss on the cheek, but a kiss on the lips with a much different message. Her admirer was starving to be in a relationship with someone and didn't care if it meant displacing Todd to get there.

Sarah didn't kiss him back, but she didn't exactly push him away. She was confused, so she thanked him and told him he should be going. After he left, Sarah sat on the couch and thought about what happened. Deep down, she was a little excited. She was also a little scared. She tried to rationalize the situation. After all, she and Todd weren't married. She wondered if he might be interested in other girls when he was traveling.

Guilt set in the next morning. She had betrayed her commitment to Todd and let someone else think there might be a chance of more to come. She decided she had made a mistake. Her heart belonged to Todd. The evening of his return, she told him they should start to think about getting married and moving out of the complex.

"What brought this on?" he asked.

"I've had some guys hitting on me lately. It's nothing, but I'm getting tired of it. It's not the best place for us anymore."

Todd doubted the reason, but accepted her assurances. He knew if it weren't these guys, there would be others. He met with Grant and Brian and mentioned asking Sarah to marry him. He was looking for their approval. Did they like her? Did they think she was the right girl for him? Did they think marriage was good for him at this point?

The answer to all his questions was a resounding, "Yes!" They thought she was the greatest woman Todd had ever dated. He would be crazy not to marry her before someone else stole her. Todd agreed, thinking of the guys in the complex.

## St. Patrick Drives out the Serpents

Two weeks later, on St. Patrick's Day, Todd popped the question. Sarah accepted. They set the date for September 17. Naturally, their parents were thrilled.

The wedding was perfect. Almost 200 of their closest friends joined in the celebration. The honeymoon was almost perfect— except that the environment reminded them of the apartment complex. Cancun was as much a pick-up place for singles as it was a honeymoon spot for newlyweds. It was, in a sense, a relational hospital. Quick medicine for what ails the soul. People went there to connect and work on the right side of the equation, but a week spent partying doesn't quite make it. Nevertheless, Todd and Sarah had a great time.

They returned to a home they had just purchased. It was in a nice subdivision in a nice part of town. Todd had done well in the first year of his new job and used his bonuses for the down payment. The yards were cared for by the homeowner's association, a plus for Todd and Sarah, who had full social calendars. They hired a cleaning lady from "Miss Minnie's Maid Service" and told all their friends they had a maid. What prestige! They had arrived!

Time passed quickly. The people they chose to associate with influenced their aspirations. Todd and Sarah had started their careers, acquired their first home, and made the money they had dreamed of as kids. They were playing the status and accomplishment game. Life couldn't be better.

## THINK IT THROUGH

*Do you get caught up in what you can accomplish and acquire? Are your goals based on acquisitions and achievements? Regardless of how much money you make, do you still strive for acquisition and achievement based on what you can afford? What happened to the people in your life as you chased that goal? Were you making friends that were in the competitive mode of outdoing each other or were they true friends like Grant and Brian? Take a look at this next period of Todd and Sarah's life, and see if you have ever experienced anything similar.*

## The Race for Acquisition and Accomplishment Accelerates

The first two years of marriage passed quickly. Todd and Sarah maintained a very busy social calendar, getting together with friends most weekends. Both were making great money and wanted everyone to know it. Todd had become the top salesman in his region. Sarah had also done well. She became a contributing editor to her newspaper and was writing her own stories. When their combined incomes reached $145,000 a year, they moved to a larger house in an affluent suburb. They bought new cars. Todd struck a deal with one his dealers to lease a brand-new BMW, and Sarah drove a convertible.

Todd and Sarah were living high and had the monthly bills to prove it. Their mortgage, car payments, credit cards, and living expenses absorbed every bit of income. But they were making ends meet and living a fast, full lifestyle.

By the sixth year of their marriage, Todd began to wonder what their next step would be. Some of their friends had started families, and that seemed interesting. They might have to cut down on their social calendars, or maybe not. Some of their friends had au pairs so they could maintain their work and social schedules.

### Another Life

"It's a girl!" Sarah cried out in elated exhaustion.

Todd's heart leapt into his throat. Anne Christine Hanson, their first child, was born. She peered into their faces through wrinkled slits of blue, and moved into their hearts to stay.

But Todd and Sarah were in for a surprise. Babies take work—lots of it. Diapers, feedings, and doctor appointments had to take first priority. This was unexpected. They were accustomed to having their own timetables and assumed their baby would naturally work effortlessly into their schedules. They had not considered they might lose sleep or have to adapt to their child's needs.

Although they didn't get much sleep, the first few months were filled with joy. But Sarah missed her job. They decided they needed to hire some help so they could get back to their old lives. A search for a nanny began, preferably someone who could live with them. Sarah was anxious to get back to work, and both yearned to go away for weekends as they had so often before their daughter was born.

Through a friend, they heard of a service that brought young women from Indonesia to work as babysitters and housekeepers. After several weeks of paperwork and research, they greeted their new live-in help. The young woman's name was Rabekah, which they shortened to "Becky." Becky spoke English very well. She came from a very poor family of nine and her entire family—parents, four sisters and two brothers— lived in a two-room pole house in a village on the outskirts of Jakarta.

The couple took full advantage of having Becky on board and immediately began taking weekend trips. They arranged their schedules so that Becky did all of the hard stuff with Anne. The moment anything got messy or Anne started to fuss, Becky would be summoned to whisk her away.

Life was so easy that Sarah and Todd decided to have another child for Anne to play with. Sixteen months after Anne was born, Sarah gave birth to Scott Cole Hanson. As soon as she was able, Sarah once again headed back to the newspaper, leaving Becky in charge of the kids and the house. In fact, Sarah put Scott on formula as soon as he was born so that Becky could do the middle-of-the-night feedings. As if nothing had happened, Sarah and Todd were getting a full night's sleep. They saw Scott and Anne mornings and evenings, although most mornings they left for work before the kids were awake. It was just the beginning of relational unconsciousness with their children.

## Chapter Summary

- Sometimes people focus so intently on acquisition and achievement they completely lose sight of the important relationships in their lives—they move into a relational coma.

- Sometimes people are so starved for the people side of the equation in their lives that they pursue bad behavior to get it. These behaviors may include extramarital affairs, unhealthy relationships at work and lopsided friendships.

- When we finally realize we've become relationally unconscious and reach the failure state (break-ups, divorces, separations) then we tip the scale in the opposite direction and focus over 90% of our attention on the relationships in our life. But often it's too late.

- We are all capable of striving for acquisition and achievement, regardless of the amount of money we make.

- We become relationally unconscious when we neglect the responsibilities we have toward others.

**POINTS TO PONDER**

- What have you strived the hardest to acquire or achieve?

  — Did it come at the expense of someone else?

- Are you out of balance in any of the relationships in your life?

- Have you become relationally unconscious with anyone in your life?

# 4

# Todd Is in a Race— and Doesn't Realize It

TODD AND SARAH continued to increase their incomes, but no matter how much they made, there was always more to strive for. Their circle of friends was full of high achievers competing to outdo each other. There was always a better car, better jewelry, better clothes, and a more extravagant vacation. They had to have something new or better than their friends or neighbors to feel good about themselves. Investing became a hot topic as well. The guys talked about what investment they had made recently and how it was doing. Even Brian and Grant had joined the race. Though not at the same income level as Todd and Sarah, they still were caught up in the excitement of who owned what—even if they couldn't really afford it.

The three old friends and their wives still socialized, but Brian saw Todd the least. Brian and his wife often admitted to each other that the Hanson lifestyle was far above theirs. Todd boasted so much that they were put off. Though Brian was Todd's lifelong friend, he began to feel inferior. Despite his high income, he was just a mechanic. Todd was a "sales executive" and flaunted his title. Brian and his wife couldn't afford to give parties or eat in trendy restaurants on the scale that Sarah and Todd did. This division widened as the years passed.

Grant, on the other hand, had done almost as well. Both sets of parents worked and had live-in help for their kids. Todd and Grant spent most of their free time together. Their unspoken competition was friendly, yet fierce. Whenever either achieved or acquired something new, he was quick to get on the phone to brag about it. Though they thought they were calling to chat as friends, deep down each knew he was challenging the other.

## THINK IT THROUGH

*Todd, Sarah, and their friends were running hard to compete; yet they never stopped to ask if this was a race they wanted to be in. Instead, Todd ran faster, unsure where the path would lead him. The left side of the equation is entirely about a race that can never be won. There is always something more to acquire and achieve.*

*Has this happened to you? Do you feel like you are in a race? Are you pleased with where you think it will take you? Do you even know where you want to end up? As you read more about Todd's life, compare it to yours.*

---

### *Are you caught up in the left side of the equation race?*

---

## A SEDUCTIVE MARATHON

Todd and Grant were competitive about their jobs, incomes, investments, houses and yards, clothing, what they drank and where they ate. They were even competitive about their kids. Parents in their group insisted the children participate in sports from the time they could walk. This was another way to show off and spend more money. The kids had designer warm-up outfits, expensive shoes and the best equipment. Some parents hired trainers.

When game day came, the parents were more excited than the kids. Each vied to out-yell the others. Some got so frustrated and competitive they'd rage at their own children for making a wrong move. The kids often left crying and mortified, convinced they were failures because they had disappointed their parents. Many really didn't want to play—if it could even be called "playing." Of course, the parents would never admit to being competitive; it was just how they expressed themselves.

---

### What are you "competitive" about?

---

The junior sport scene kept Todd involved for a number of years, but then he needed something new. Todd and Grant started going to the gym together and discovered that every good-looking single woman in town worked out there. All those well-toned bodies in skimpy exercise outfits. What an unbelievable spectacle. Both men were out of shape and self-conscious about how they looked, but soon found their physical appearance didn't matter. As long as they had money and showed an interest in women, an abundance of beauties competed for their attention. Never before had so many women made such open advances.

It was the attention they were after. They longed for the *Right Side of the Equation*. They had personal needs that weren't being met. Somehow they had stopped pursuing, pleasing and meeting the needs of the people already in their lives and vice versa. It caused them to think they could fill their need for the *Right Side of the Equation* through other people. They were going from relationally unconscious to relationally stupid.

## Passionate Passages

About half the women at the gym were divorced or separated and had become desperate to find another someone for companionship. The other half were unhappily married, eager to find a companion that found them desirable again. Then it happened.

Todd had a successful day. He'd landed a really big deal and he was ready to celebrate. Several colleagues were having drinks in the lounge of the hotel. He joined them, ordering a gin and tonic. Several drinks and stories later, he found himself in bed with Terry, a woman he'd met at the gym who also worked at Regency. This was the start of an ongoing affair. Each felt totally safe in the relationship, because neither wanted to leave their spouse and they lived far enough apart not to see each other frequently. Then one day she announced that Todd was the guy for her. She would leave her husband, and Todd must leave his wife.

Todd was stunned. Though his marriage wasn't perfect, he was comfortable with Sarah. A divorce would cripple him, both emotionally and financially. Emotionally because he saw it as a failure and didn't want to be perceived by anyone as a failure. Financially because he wouldn't be able to afford the lifestyle he had grown accustomed while having to support two families. His alarm turned to terror when the lady insisted, threatening to go public about their affair. At the very least, both of them would probably be fired.

He realized their relationship had to end. She could tell his wife, he told her, because he intended to do so anyway. And if she chose to inform their boss, that was okay too, though it might cost them their jobs. He convinced her that their affair was over. Then he waited nervously for the vengeance of an angry woman.

He was luckier than he knew he deserved. She decided to cut her losses and do nothing. Still, Todd confessed to Sarah. He wasn't prepared for her response. She, he learned, had been having an affair with one of his friends. Both agreed to try to salvage their marriage. The following months were extremely difficult. Both felt cheated and guilty at the same time. Trust was gone. They realized they were searching for fulfillment, but didn't know how to get it from each other.

## PARTY HARDER

They were soon to find themselves in worse shape. Todd dulled his emptiness with alcohol. He and Sarah had lived a party life for fifteen years, so it was easy to drink a little more. He'd often stop on the way home after work for a few drinks with his buddies. Once he got home, he would drink even more with dinner. He didn't know it yet, but he had failed to fulfill the *Right Side of the Equation*, so he simply checked out.

Todd and Sarah both tried to block out thoughts of the affairs and how messed up life had become. Their desire for fulfillment from other lovers competed with their outrage at being betrayed by someone they trusted. It was all too confusing. Instead, they tried to keep busy at work and with outside interests, hoping time would offer perspective.

They threw themselves into their jobs and activities at their new country club. However, the club brought a new set of problems and another level of competition. That was okay. Both were used to vying for position. The club's membership was a Who's Who for the area. Every prominent businessman was a member. There was old money and new money, spent on golf carts, expensive clubs, and lessons to bring down the handicap.

It was easy to get involved in something new and forget the

pain of the past. Todd thought that happiness might be found with belonging to the club. Their intense schedule provided a positive public façade, but inside they felt empty. They were together and doing the same things, but any semblance they had of a loving relationship was gone. They separated themselves from their kids. Anne and Scott were now in high school and like many teenagers, wanted nothing to do with their parents. Todd and Sarah were so involved with their group of friends that they barely noticed.

As usual, they had a live-in housekeeper who was supposed to look after the kids. The kids claimed they didn't need looking after and did what they wanted. They got everything they wanted. As long as they brought home reasonable grades and stayed out of trouble, Mom and Dad didn't bother them. They were doing exactly what Todd had done when he was in high school. They partied every weekend and some weeknights. The only difference was they had more money.

Of course, Todd and Sarah thought they were ideal parents. They bought their kids whatever they needed and then some. They gave them lots of freedom. They didn't bother them when they wanted to go out or bring friends over, even when Todd and Sarah were out of town, which was quite often. Out-of-town nights turned into big party nights for Anne and Scott. They would tell the housekeeper to take the night off and have all their friends over for the drinking and drugs. Though Todd and Sarah set rules, Anne and Scott quickly learned to work the system. They had parents who hadn't a clue what they were doing.

## Strike Three—and He Didn't Even Know He Was Out

Todd had tried it all. He had accomplished his career goals, had acquired every possession he had ever dreamed of, and had experimented with different relationships. Yet it still didn't dawn on him that he was going from one thing to another without any true fulfillment. He had no plan or purpose for the decisions he was making. He certainly wasn't following any rules. He had no idea there was an equation that could be followed to be successful. But that was about to change. Todd was about to meet someone who would change his life—someone who would enlighten him about the *Right Side of the Equation*.

Could you be looking for the same thing?

---

*Are you looking for a change in your life?*

---

## Chapter Summary

- The quest for acquisition and achievement can divide family relationships and friendships.

- Society can cause us to think that buying more will make us happier.

- Acquisition and achievement can become your only link to relationships with other people- when you call them to tell them what you've acquired or accomplished.

- The quest for more is insatiable. The more you get the more you want.

- At some point, we all will crave the *Right Side of the Equation*.

- Sometimes we think the relationships we already have can be bettered, so we look elsewhere in an unhealthy way.

- When we can't fulfill the *Right Side of the Equation*, we may turn to the things we think we can control, such as acquisition and achievement.

- Sometimes we replace the *Right Side of the Equation* with work, television, hobbies and sometimes drugs or alcohol.

## POINTS TO PONDER

- Do you ever buy things you can't really afford?
  - If yes, why?
  - Is it to keep up with appearances?
  - Is it because acquisition and achievement feel good?
  - Is that acquisition and achievement ever truly fulfilling?
- Have you ever let financial ability come between you and someone else?
- When relationships in your life have not gone well, what have you replaced it with?

# 5

# An Irresistible Offer

TODD HAD BEEN WITH THE AUTO PARTS COMPANY for over nineteen years. He became a regional vice-president in charge of fifteen regions. His area was continually the top producer in the country, and Todd was doing extremely well financially. He had his job so wired it was second nature. His life was on autopilot.

Then one day Todd was invited to lunch with Severson Systems, one of the major manufacturers his company represented. He assumed this was one of the usual "you're doing a great job for us" lunches. It turned out, however, to be a recruiting lunch. Besides President Blake Severson II, the marketing and operations vice presidents were also present. Todd learned they were considering him for Regional Sales Manager, a position similar to his current job and one he knew he could do well. Todd was offered other jobs in the past, but turned them down. He was comfortable where he was. But what caught Todd's interest was an idea Mr. Severson explained that resonated within him.

"A job with us, Hanson," he boasted, "isn't about money or climbing ladders. It's about Relational Intelligence. We've found that when we strive to understand what all parties want and need and then seek to fulfill them, everyone thrives. Our customers want something more than just our product. Our employees want something more than just collecting a paycheck. Our spouses want something more than just a roommate. Our kids want something more than just a parental dictator. Everyone wants something more than what you think they are there for.

"We've learned that employees want to do well in their position while enjoying the people they work with. They want others to be what I call, 'relationally intelligent.' We've developed a very specific program to teach people how to do this through a program entitled, the *Right Side of the Equation*. When people become relationally intelligent, they become content in their work and their personal lives."

Blake went on to explain more about the program and why Severson Systems was flourishing. Todd was skeptical but intrigued. He thought it deserved further investigation and agreed to take a deeper look at the company. He thanked his hosts and scheduled a full-day appointment the following week at their factory.

Todd left the lunch contemplating this thing called Relational Intelligence. All his life he had focused on his own achievements and position—professionally, socially and financially. The thought never crossed his mind that customers might want more than buying his products. He was perplexed by the notion that his wife and kids might want something more. It made sense on one level, because he felt he wanted something more from his family as well. But what exactly he wanted or could give was a mystery.

He wanted to talk about his lunch with someone, but whom? He decided to call Sarah at her office. She was surprised to get a call from him during the day and even more surprised to hear that he was interested in a new job. Things were stable and profitable for him at Regent Wholesale. Why change now?

Over dinner that night, Todd told Sarah how Blake Severson had caught his interest by the way he described his company's success. Todd knew that Severson Systems was extremely profitable. He knew all the top brass made very handsome incomes.

In the past, Todd had won elaborate trips offered as sales promotion prizes by Severson Systems. Todd and Sarah met Mr. Severson and many of the company's regional managers on these excursions. They even speculated about what contributed to Severson System's success. Todd knew that the person he might be replacing made a respectable income, certainly more than Todd was currently earning for doing essentially the same job.

Sarah listened as Todd explained Relational Intelligence. "Blake explained that people want something more than just doing business. Employees want more than a paycheck, customers want more than products to purchase. Then he talked about how we want more from the relationships in our personal lives. Severson said he had a specific plan in place to achieve this. I would have to learn and implement this plan."

## Why Are They Smiling?

The following week, Todd spent a day at Severson Systems headquarters. He was greeted with a sign that read, "Severson Systems Welcomes Todd Hanson"—a nice touch that immediately made him feel comfortable and significant.

"Mr. Severson will be right with you," the receptionist said with a smile. She offered him something to drink and a binder with his name printed on the front—another nice touch, he thought. Inside was literature about the company, an organizational chart, and a section with what appeared to be several company policies and memos to their employees. He learned quite a bit about Severson Systems in the next few minutes before Mr. Severson appeared.

"Hey, Todd, how ya doing? Great to have you here!" He suggested Todd call him Blake and asked if he'd looked over the day's agenda in his notebook. Todd hadn't seen that sheet and quickly pulled it out. The day began with an introduction to the administrative offices, then a plant tour, followed by lunch with Mr. Severson and golf with key personnel.

Mr. Severson started by introducing the receptionist and went systematically through the 25 people in the administrative offices. Todd thought this seemed like a small staff for a company that annually grossed $152 million. He noticed the atmosphere was relaxed, cordial. No one seemed to be working hard at all.

The employees called Mr. Severson "Blake," and he introduced people by saying something about their personal lives along with a compliment for what they'd done for the company. Todd was a bit skeptical about the overt friendliness. Was Severson putting on a front to impress him? Did he really believe every person was doing that great a job? Was he sincerely interested in their personal lives? If it was genuine, Todd thought it was pretty cool. But still he was somewhat skeptical. He needed to learn more before he could believe that Blake Severson actually had that kind of relationship with his employees.

Next they toured the factory, which was across the street from the administrative offices. Blake introduced Todd to the employees at each workstation and people they passed. Again he'd mention something about the employee's family or personal interests and make a comment about a recent work achievement for nearly everyone they encountered.

Todd was marveling to himself how well kept the factory looked when Blake commented that everyone in the factory took great pride in running a clean operation. The factory supervisor was meticulous about having systems in place that required everything to be in exact order.

They visited the shipping area where Todd noticed something else unusual. It appeared the entire administrative staff had crossed the street to pack boxes! Blake explained that a customer had an emergency and needed a large order shipped within the next few hours. Almost every administrator and supervisor Todd met was now putting boxes into cases and cases onto pallets. What's more, they looked like they were having a good time!

Blake indicated that when anything extraordinary came up, everyone pitched in to get it done. He rarely had to ask, for people naturally sensed the need and acted upon it.

They returned to Blake's office where lunch had been set up at a small corner table. The room was large and friendly with many photos of Blake's family and company employees. While they ate, Blake asked Todd a series of deliberate questions to assess his abilities and attitude. He further asked if he had a set of written goals for work and home, to which Todd indicated he only had written goals at Regency. Blake asked how he ran his sales division at Regency, how many employees reported to him, and about his management style to see if Todd had the competency to take the job. Blake then described the program he had implemented at Severson Systems, the *Right Side of the Equation*. He was mainly looking to see if Todd was teachable. Was he open to the Right Side and could he implement it?

## INTRODUCING THE RIGHT SIDE OF THE EQUATION

"The program I've developed has many attributes of a game," Blake illustrated. "It is responsible for the success we've experienced at Severson Systems and for the happiness and accomplishment of every employee here, including me.

"I tell people the program has many of the same attributes of a game because most understand the concept. Games typically include a purpose and method for playing, rules, and players. Our program is no different. It has a purpose, rules, players and a defined method to how we enact the program similar to the play of the game. The object of our program is to master Relational Intelligence. If you choose to join Severson Systems," Blake added, "you will have to learn how to deploy the program in your own department and will need to learn what it means to be relationally intelligent, too."

"How will I learn this program?" Todd asked.

Blake said he personally would do most of the teaching, but that other employees might fill in from time to time. The first several weeks would be spent on the fundamentals of the program and the rules. Blake added that these could become some of the most important concepts Todd will ever hear.

"You may have heard the term 'the game of life,'" Blake began. "We are all in this game. Most people think they are playing when they just show up, even though they haven't a clue about the rules or ultimate purpose. That's what I call, 'playing in the default mode'—and it is the cause of relational unconsciousness. For example, take professional sports or business. Both have very detailed plans and strategies that participants practice every day. Now ask anyone if such a plan exists for his or her personal life. Most will give you that 'deer in the headlights' look. Most individuals don't have a deliberate plan that clearly articulates their goals and objectives, which I call the left side of the equation, and what they need to do to meet those goals and objectives, which I call the *Right Side of the Equation*. Ultimate success will be determined by the *Right Side of the Equation*. How well people understand their role, responsibility, contribution and interaction with each other is paramount to reaching the goals and objectives. In simple terms, you can't achieve any goals or objectives without others.

"But there's more. We've found that how well those people behave and interact as a team plays a major role in the outcome and our overall success. I've determined there are five essential characteristics people must have to be a successful part of any team. I call these characteristics The Five Cs. They are Character, Competency, Chemistry, Capability and Contribution. I learned the first three, Character, Competency and Chemistry, from Bill Hybels of Willow Creek Church during a leadership conference. These were good, but I believe two other characteristics are crucial for success—Capability and Contribution. You can have people who are competent, have great character, create good chemistry, but if they are incapable of doing their job because something is going on in their life, they are useless.

"Todd, the *Right Side of the Equation* takes the game of life and kicks it up several notches. It adds purpose for playing and a specific plan to achieve the homerun that comes from true fulfillment. The key component is having people around you who do what you expect and vice versa. That can only happen when you have a process to align the needs and expectations of all parties. This is Relational Intelligence. First, you must understand what those needs are. Most companies are focused solely on their goals and fail to remember they need people to succeed. At some point, almost everyone becomes relationally unconscious. That's when we lose sense of the people around us and their needs. We at Severson Systems care for our employees, meeting their professional needs so they are thus capable of helping the company succeed."

As Todd pondered what he was hearing, Blake explained further. "Todd, the great thing about this program is that I can always tell whether our employees are 'in the game' or not. If they are in, their lives continually improve and they will be fulfilled. I know when people aren't following the program. They don't perform as well and they are usually unhappy or depressed; definitely not living fulfilled lives."

Blake pointed at Todd's chair. "Most people who've sat where you're sitting now don't know what to think at this point," he said. "It's okay if you don't fully grasp it, but I can tell you it works. We are succeeding because our employees truly love working here. I'd say that perhaps all of them are satisfied employees. They are able to reach some of their lifelong goals, and at the same time become more productive and profitable. This is a combination I think every person and every company is looking for."

## Impressing the Boss

Blake switched gears. Now he wanted to learn more about Todd, especially about his family. What were his interests? Todd started with a brief overview of his career—how in his first year as a regional salesman he became the top producer for his area. He described the dollar volumes he had reached over the years and each of his responsibilities as he moved up the ladder to Regional Sales Manager.

"What about your family?" asked Blake. Todd mentioned he had been married to Sarah for eighteen years and briefly described her career and the advancements she had made as a journalist. Blake recognized her name, which made Todd proud. Then Todd described his two children as "typical high schoolers, mostly doing their own thing these days with their friends."

Todd was eager to return to what he thought would really

impress Severson. He described all the things that wowed his buddies—his housekeeper, memberships at the local gym and a prestigious country club. He described his elite biker club and some of the road trips they took each year. Finally, to be sure Blake knew how well he had done, he told him about his stock portfolio.

Blake then asked Todd to describe his typical week. Great! Another chance to impress. He stressed the long hours he worked to show what a devoted employee he was. But life wasn't all work. He spent weekends at the club playing golf, followed by dinner there. He did his thing, Sarah had her interests and the kids did what they wanted, too. Each of them typically went separate ways.

"And what do you do on Sundays?" Sundays, Todd explained, were typically for his Harley motorcycle group. They visited other clubs or rode on day trips. It was an opportunity for him and the guys to get away, but occasionally they brought their wives. At the end of his impressive discourse on his achievements, Todd was satisfied that he had done a splendid job of impressing his potential boss.

Blake was unimpressed, although the answers had been more or less what he expected. Todd was relationally uncon-scious. Severson Systems could bring great value to his life. The real question in Blake's mind was whether Todd could bring value to Severson Systems.

"Why would you consider a position at Severson?" Blake in-quired. This put Todd in a competitive mode. As Todd calculated his response, Blake suggested he answer from his heart, not what he thought Blake wanted to hear. What did that mean? After some thought Todd decided to be as honest as possible.

"Blake," he confessed, "there's something interesting going on here. I'm not exactly sure what it is, but it's different from most companies. My wife and I noticed it before on one of your sales promotion trips. It intrigues and attracts me. I'm very comfortable where I am and never thought I would consider leaving, but I just get the sense that something's out there that I'm missing. I don't know exactly how to explain it."

Blake smiled. A homerun answer. He told Todd he completely understood the feelings he was having. Severson Systems was more than building products and making profits. Their unique methods were what brought both employees and customers to the company and certainly what kept them there. Blake checked his watch and realized almost two hours had elapsed. They had a tee time at the golf course and should go. In the lobby, four men and two women were waiting for them.

Surprisingly, the golf course was public, though it was considered one of the best in the area. Todd had assumed Blake belonged to a private club. Then he noticed Blake's clubs. Not bad, but not one of the $2,000 sets he had expected.

They split into two foursomes, agreeing to switch around after the ninth hole so Todd could meet all six people. The three people Todd started with included the company's accounting and production managers, as well as the operations vice president he had met at the recruiting lunch.

None in Todd's party played exceptionally well. In fact, they were pretty bad, though they seemed to be enjoying themselves. They played once in a while with customers and other employees, they told Todd. It gave them a chance to get to know people outside the office setting.

The production manager chatted with Todd about a variety of things, none directly related to production. He talked about the team he worked with and how gifted they were. He mentioned things they did together outside of work, like fishing and hunting trips, birthday parties, and NASCAR races.

The Severson people asked Todd a variety of questions unrelated to work. He tried to impress them as he did his regular group of friends. He was obviously a better golfer, so he let each of them know how they could improve their game.

At the end of nine holes, the groups switched. Besides Blake, Todd was now playing with the national sales manager, the man who would be Todd's boss if he was offered the job. The fourth in their party was an assembly line worker. Todd thought it strange this man had come along. What could he have in common with everyone else? But as they worked their way around the course, Todd observed that no one seemed to mind.

The two new members of the second foursome asked about Todd's family and interests, not what he thought he could bring to their company. And, as with the first nine holes, Todd outplayed them all. Nevertheless, all seemed to enjoy themselves and made sure Todd did as well.

They finished up around 5:30. Todd was surprised they were anxious to get home instead of going to the bar or back to the office. Blake saw Todd to his car, promising to touch base in the next few days. He asked Todd to look over the material in the binder, especially some of the "Ethical Exercises." Blake explained that the Ethical Exercises were the basis for discussions employees have on a regular basis that are centered on the rules the company followed.

On the way home, Todd stopped at his country club for a few drinks with his buddies. Grant was there and Todd shared briefly about the day's events. He didn't describe the questions Blake asked or the *Right Side of the Equation*. Todd still hadn't fully grasped what Blake was talking about. Grant encouraged Todd

THE RIGHT SIDE OF THE EQUATION

to take the job if it was offered, based on the good things he had heard about Severson Systems.

When Todd returned home, he tried explaining Blake's *Right Side of the Equation* to Sarah. After dinner, he opened the binder and read through some of the materials, including the group of pages labeled "Ethical Exercises."

## BLAKE'S REPORT CARD

The next day, Blake Severson met with the same six co-workers who played golf with Todd. He asked each to make a list of Todd's strengths and weaknesses putting them in weighted priority order. Each list rated the positives as important, while the weaknesses seemed repairable with time and training. On the positive side, they agreed that Todd was probably an honest person who wanted to do the right thing. He was devoted and loyal to the company he worked for, and was married for eighteen years. Their lists of his weaknesses were almost identical. All felt he was eager to impress. They could see he had lived a life based on acquisition and achievement and hadn't been exposed to the *Right Side of the Equation*. Based on their conversations on the golf course, they suspected he didn't have great relationships with his wife or kids. He might even have stayed married for appearances, since his wife was so well known, or to avoid the financial disruption of a divorce. They were very perceptive.

Blake agreed with most of these observations. No surprises. Then he asked if they thought Todd would make it as part of the Severson team. The position was open, and Todd had the competency they were looking for. He was well established in the community and would likely stay with the company for another 15-20 years. It appeared to the team that Todd had character. In spite of some of his faults, he was a likable guy. There was chemistry between them. Based on Todd's track record, they knew he could make a contribution. It didn't appear there was anything standing in the way of his capability to perform in the job. It appeared he encompassed the "Five Cs" and would be a good choice.

The employees had seen many lives changed as they learned to apply the *Right Side of the Equation*. They decided to give Blake the "thumbs up" for Todd to come on board—provided Todd was willing to go through the normal Severson training process. Blake concurred.

The next day, Blake met with Todd and told him the group felt he had promise. The job was his if he agreed to go through the training sessions and learn to apply the program in his life. Severson Systems had a probationary period that gauged each new employee's ability to follow the company's systems and the program. Todd's new financial package was similar to his old one, with normal incentives every sales position holds.

## A FATEFUL DECISION

Todd decided to take the job. Employees seemed to love working there. The company had an aura of success and a level of satisfaction that he hadn't seen anywhere else. Todd casually talked with a few customers and they agreed Severson Systems had the relational component that had earned them an excellent reputation. One company stated it was the first time they had ever worked with another company that actually showed them what Relational Intelligence looked like. Todd was excited about what the future would hold for him.

*What does Relational Intelligence mean to you?*

When Todd got home, he was almost embarrassed to tell Sarah he had accepted the job. He wasn't going to do any better financially unless he performed at an extraordinary level. He couldn't explain why he left one company after 19 years to take a job that felt better. He ended up telling his wife, kids, and friends that it was an advancement of sorts. He was now a regional sales manager with a manufacturer instead of a supplier. It sounded like another achievement that could boost his ego.

He gave notice at Regent, explaining he was taking a position with one of the companies they represented. He agreed to make himself fully available after he left and could stay a few weeks to train someone if necessary.

It was important for Todd to leave Regent on good terms because he would continue to have almost daily involvement with them. They were an integral part of his region and could provide a big part of his future income. Naturally they were surprised and disappointed after so many years, though it wasn't unusual for people to leave. Regent fostered a competitive "climbing the ladder" philosophy.

**Chapter Summary**

- People want something more
than the obvious.

  — Customers want more than a product.

  — Employees want more than a paycheck.

  — Married couples want more
  than roommates.

  — Kids want more than a roof over
  their heads and food on the table.

  — Friends and family want more
  than just your presence.

- The *Right Side of the Equation* helps
us determine what people want
and how to meet their needs.

- When we stop thinking about the wants
and needs of the people around us, we
become relationally unconscious.

- Relational Intelligence is when we
continually strive to understand and meet
the needs of the people around us.

- When we are relationally intelligent, people
around us will help meet our own needs.

## POINTS TO PONDER

- Do you want more than just a paycheck at work?

- Do you want something more from your marriage?

- Do you want a deeper relationship with your kids?

- Would you say you are relationally unconscious or relationally intelligent?

  — If the latter, what are you doing on a daily basis to prove it?

# 6

# Learning the Right Side of the Equation

TODD STARTED HIS NEW POSITION in February. The first week was spent setting up his office and getting to know the people within his region. In addition to three months of product-line training, he began the *Right Side of the Equation* training through weekly meetings with Blake. He would learn the program during the first month and then live out the program from that point on.

Todd went to Blake's office for their first training session. He wasn't sure what to expect. Blake handed him an overview of the program. "Let me explain the *Right Side of the Equation* program to you. I gave you a brief overview of the game and Relational Intelligence at lunch a few weeks ago. Now I want to explain it in detail. As you can see on the card, there are three components to the program:

1    Goals and Objectives: Describes what we will accomplish.

2    People and Relationships: Will determine how we will accomplish it and with whom.

3    Rules: Guidelines we must follow as we accomplish it.

Left side of the equation     Right side of the equation

**OBJECTIVE**     **RELATIONSHIPS**

**GOALS**     **PEOPLE**

**RULES**

"As you can see from the card, Goals and Objectives are the left side of the equation. My experience is that nearly everyone has some kind of goal or objective for some part of life. For example, most people between 18 and 30 have a goal to get married, find a place to live, buy a car, etc. Most companies have internal goals and objectives. They also have goals and objectives they hope to reach with their customers. Many people have goals and objectives for their families and themselves. Sometimes these goals and objectives are written down and well defined; other times they are mental thoughts and images. Either way, the goals get the majority of our attention. In many cases people focus over 90% of their time, talent and energy on goals.

"The *Right Side of the Equation* is about people. This is where the Five Cs come into play. It's not just that we need people to meet our goals and objectives. These people must have the right Character, Competency, Chemistry, Capability and Contribution to really be successful. Character, Competency and Chemistry are prerequisites for the *Right Side of the Equation* to become effective. Capability and Contribution are keys to sustaining success. More importantly, being able to properly assess Capability and Contribution to provide the right feedback is essential. Articulating and aligning expectations is a major component to this. Our program gives us the framework and process for how we do this."

Todd interjected to clarify his understanding. "This is the Relational Intelligence you mentioned before?"

"Exactly," Blake replied. "Now, the rules part of the program provides the necessary guidelines we must follow to make sure we behave in a way everyone expects. You see, every employee here, our customers and our vendors have expectations of the way we do business. They expect us to live out the Five Cs along with them. The rules define what our behavior should be."

Blake leaned in, stressing the importance of his next comment. "Todd, it's imperative you understand this program applies to more than our work environment. Everything you will learn applies to your personal life as well. You have ideas of how you want your personal life to go. Unless you understand how it's going to work from a people point of view, it won't come out the way you think it will. When we understand our goals and then can articulate and align expectations with the people around us, especially at home, things change for the better. Here's the deal, Todd. If you want to be successful in life, you have to work on the *Right Side of the Equation* in everything you do. In fact, you'll find your personal life is where you live the program first. Each week I will give you homework assignments to practice with your family."

---

*If you want to be successful in life, you must work on the right side of the equation in everything.*

---

Todd had never envisioned learning something at work that he would take home to his family. He needed to think this through. He wasn't sure he wanted to be required to take initiatives from work home to his family. He was apprehensive about this aspect of his new job, but decided to give it a try for a few weeks.

Blake continued, "We will spend the next six weeks going over the program. First we'll discuss its purpose. Then we will look at the three components in greater detail: goals and objectives, people and relationships, and finally the rules. Then we will go over the most important part—how you live this out in every area of your life."

## THE REASON: THREE MOST IMPORTANT THINGS

"This program developed out of need. Several years ago I had two dilemmas in my life that surfaced at the same time. The first was a problem with my business. I couldn't attract and retain lower wage earners. They took other jobs for as little as ten cents more per hour. It was expensive and both mentally and physically exhausting to continually replace these folks. The second dilemma was personal; although it may have been caused by frustration from the first problem. I reached a point where I wondered why am I here and what was I supposed to accomplish," Blake confided. "I didn't merely ask myself why I was here at Severson Systems or what I hoped to accomplish in my business. I asked why I was here on this earth. What did I hope to accomplish in my life? I wanted to understand my purpose both professionally and personally. As I pondered this question and tried to sort out the problem at work, it came to me that the first thing I needed to do was identify what was important to me. Then, perhaps, I could build upon my priorities. I spent a considerable amount of time identifying what were the most important things in my life.

"At the same time, I studied everything I could find on employee retention and motivation. It didn't take long to learn this topic had been studied regularly since the 1940's. Every study I found had the same top four or five answers for retaining employees. The number one thing people wanted in the workplace was to enjoy those they worked with. Number two was to fulfill the contract. This meant they wanted to give an hour of their time, talent, and expertise in exchange for a dollar amount. People wanted to actually produce something for their earnings. Third was fair treatment—the same set of rules for everyone. Fourth was appreciation for the job they had done, and fifth was money. If they didn't get numbers 1–3, then money became number one. It dawned on me that perhaps the solutions to my work problems could also apply to my personal struggles. What people wanted in their workplace were the same things I determined were the most important things in my own life. I then built this program as a method of integrating those things into my life and the lives of every employee here. My solution solved both problems."

"That's great," responded Todd.

"As I began to share the process I went through to determine what was important in my life, I found others essentially came up with the same top three. There was a pattern—I was on to something," he shared with a smile. "Once I found a way to integrate my solution into both my professional and personal life, things changed. Every one of our employees has implemented these three priorities into his or her life. My wife and children have too. Here's how to start:

1   Identify the three most important things in your life.

2   Integrate them into every aspect of daily living, both professional and personal—via the *Right Side of the Equation* program."

Todd raised his eyebrows. "Sounds easy enough. I don't suppose you'll give me any hints as to what the top three are," he teased.

Blake chuckled. "I don't want to tell you the answers I came up with for the company and myself until you determine your own priorities. When you do, I think you will begin to see why you're here at Severson, how we'll help you reach your purpose and how you will help us reach ours. Everyone has to know they have a purpose. When you can live it every day, life becomes highly satisfying. The program will guide your efforts. We've learned that without the disciplines of a program like this, one tends to live in the default mode with no real purpose."

"You wing it," added Todd.

"Exactly. So here's how I want you to identify what's really important to you. If you had to name the three most important things in your life, what would they be? Determine what these are by thinking about three different scenarios. First, if you were stranded on a desert island with sufficient food, water, and shelter, what other three things would you choose to have with you on the island? Or say you were on a mission to another planet and as with the island, the necessities of life have been provided (food, water, shelter, and you have your health), what other three things would you take? Finally, if you were the last living person on earth, but again had plenty of food, water and shelter, what three things would you choose to have with you? Think of it as three wishes. And choose things that are applicable in all three scenarios. That's your homework."

## THREE HELPFUL TESTS

Blake further suggested that Todd weigh possible answers by running three separate tests:

- The Conscience test: This is a feeling you get inside when you make a big decision. Does it feel right or does it present that twinge of "something's wrong with it?" We all have the ability to decipher right from wrong and our conscience, if allowed, will usually confirm our decision.

- The Announcement test: Can you announce your decision to the world, including your co-workers, friends, and family, and have them applaud

you? This assumes you are announcing your
decision to people who have moral integrity.

- The Profit test: This test evaluates who wins. If
all parties involved win, it's most likely a good
decision. If you win at the expense of someone
else, it's not a good decision. If someone else
wins at your expense, it's not a good decision.

"We call this the CAP test, named after the first letter of each test
to help us remember it. It's our code for determining if we have
followed the rules. And we know that if we run all our decisions
through the test, we will live different and better lives. I want you
to make sure your decision makes sense over time. If you were to
think ahead a year, five years, or 50 years, can you look back and
believe the decisions you made were good ones? If you were on
that island for 50 years or even if you were on your death bed on
that island, would the three things you listed still make sense?"

Todd thought back over his life and some of the things he
had done. He quickly realized that many things he had done
wouldn't pass the CAP test. And they haven't turned out to be
good decisions in the long run. He pondered for a second how
things might have gone had he known of the CAP test.

---

*What happens when you run the CAP test on your own life?*

---

Blake encouraged Todd to go home and spend some time thinking about his answers. He also asked Todd to run the same questions by his family. He suggested they determine the three most
important things in their lives by evaluating what they would

pick in the same scenarios. It would be a good way to have more interaction with them, and he could pass on some good information at the same time. He saw Todd to the door and agreed to meet again on Monday to go over his answers.

That evening, Todd arrived home earlier than usual. Everyone was practically kicked out of the Severson offices by 5:00 and told to go home to their families. For the first week, this felt so strange that Todd had stopped each night at his club for a few drinks, reaching home at his "normal" time between 7:00 and 8:00 PM. Tonight was different. He was eager to get home and think through his answers about what was important to him.

Sarah and the kids were still out, and it was the maid's night off. He was alone in an eerily quiet house. He started a fire, poured a glass of wine, and sat down to consider various solutions. He thought about Blake's different scenarios and about the CAP test. Would he want some material things like his motorcycle or some of his shotguns for hunting or perhaps his car or his clothes or maybe his watch? Golf clubs? As he thought through each one, he began to think how stupid some of them might seem when scrutinized by the announcement to the world test and by the profit test. Only Todd profited. His conscience almost immediately told him they were not very important things nor would they make sense over time. From a practical standpoint there may be no gas for his motorcycle, or no paved roads. Clothes might not be necessary for survival. Maybe there would be nothing to shoot, or he could run out of ammunition. The golf clubs would provide little recreation if he didn't have a course. Even if he did, it would be boring to play by himself.

After going over a list of everything he owned or could own, he realized he would be lonely. What he would want most was someone to talk to! He contemplated each of his friends in turn.

Who would be the best choice? Then he spotted a picture of Sarah and his kids. Instantly, he knew his wife had to be his first choice. He thought about their 18 years of marriage and the many things they had done and been through together. Although they had made many mistakes, he still loved her. They were committed to each other—though perhaps for some of the wrong reasons, like how expensive a divorce would be. Still, he enjoyed her company and continued to find her attractive.

He thought back to the day Anne was born and how close he felt with Sarah and his new baby. It felt good to be a family. He had been so happy with his wife and little girl. He remembered how proud he felt when Scott was born. He thought about all of the games they went to with their kids and the many trips he and Sarah took together. They had spent so much time together. As he considered the years ahead, he even thought about death. Who would he want with him as he was dying? An image flashed into his mind—Sarah and the children by his side. They would provide the most comfort and support. And he couldn't leave out his mother, bringing the same comfort she had when he was a child. Yep, no doubt about it. In all the situations that Blake had described—the desert island, the interplanetary journey, being the last person on earth—his family would be one of the three most important things to have. In fact, they were the most important things in his life. What about his closest friends? He listed them at number two. These answers seemed as though they would pass the CAP tests as he ran through them and they made sense over time.

Todd suddenly realized he had spent over an hour contemplating this question. It was probably one of the deepest he had ever considered. Until he met Blake Severson, he had never felt a need to think about anything like this.

## THE FAMILY DEBATES THE QUESTION

As each of his family members arrived home, he asked that they eat dinner together that evening. The kids were mad. It was Friday, and they had plans with their friends. Todd told them to postpone their plans and stick around for dinner. Sarah thought it was unusual, but kind of nice. As they sat down, Todd showed them the program outline and explained each of the three components as Blake had. Though they didn't understand much about the program, they appeared somewhat interested.

Then Todd moved their focus to the most important things question. The kids rolled their eyes, sure that dad had flipped out. "I'm serious," Todd countered. He described the three settings Blake had mentioned—the desert island, the interplanetary expedition, or being the last living thing on earth. If they were guaranteed all the basics for survival—food, water, and shelter—what three things would be most important to them that would be applicable in such different situations? He asked them to write down their answers and then described the CAP test for evaluating those answers.

"What answers popped into your head when I first asked this question?" Todd asked. Scott said he immediately thought of his laptop computer so he could access any information he needed. He thought further and decided he would like some female companionship. He'd bring his girlfriend. Finally, he decided a gun for protection would be important.

Todd asked him to put his answers through the CAP test. Deep down, does a gun makes sense? Could his answers appear in the morning newspaper and would the readers applaud him?

If he were stranded on an island, what good would his laptop do, especially if he couldn't connect to the Internet or keep it powered up? Even if he had everything on his hard drive and a solar-powered battery, would everyone profit from him choosing it? Or would he stockpile computer games to satisfy his own interests? The relativity of space and time might make it hard to e-mail friends in a different solar system.

Anne said she'd want to have her CD collection. She amended this to "music" which, she was sure, would pass the CAP test. Surely no one would disapprove of music.

Next, Anne said, she'd want her photo albums.

"Why not the people instead of their pictures?" asked Scott.

"Great idea," Anne agreed. "All my friends can come along. And my family—except Scott." She and her brother exchanged sibling sneers. "And, third, I'd want a tool kit with a full set of craft supplies—needles, drills and screwdrivers so I could always be making something. That would be both practical and creative."

"I've only thought of two things," Sarah told them. "What are your three answers, Todd?"

Todd hedged. He didn't want to admit he also had only two answers. A third still eluded him. "I don't want to influence you," he told her. "I'll share my first two now. When you have a third, I'll tell you my third." His first was family, he said. This included their extended family—siblings, parents, cousins, aunts, uncles, etc. Second were their friends. Both passed the CAP test.

"I have exactly the same answers," Sarah said. For third place, she was considering books. She had a large library and loved reading. She felt books could pass the CAP test.

Todd thought books were a great idea. He'd make that his choice too! The family debated their answers for about an hour, the first serious discussion they'd ever had as a family.

When the exchange finally slowed, Anne and Scott suddenly remembered their commitments for the evening and took off. Todd and Sarah continued talking.

## TODD'S FIRST LIST

When Monday came, Todd was eager to tell Blake Severson the answers he came up with. Blake first explained that Todd's answers would eventually become his personal keys to obtaining and maintaining success and happiness. They are foundational to his purpose for deploying the program in his personal and professional life. If Todd focused on what had the most value for him, and if these things possessed true value, a purposeful and fulfilling life would become inevitable.

Todd made sure he logged Blake's comments in his brain. He sensed this was important to remember. He brought out his list.

## THE MOST IMPORTANT THINGS TO YOU

1  Family

2  Friends

3  Books

His first answer was family. Blake expressed pleasant surprise. Until then, nothing Todd had said or done indicated they were his priority. He asked Todd how he arrived at that decision. Todd described all the scenarios he had considered. On an island, out in space or on his deathbed, none of his possessions mattered. He had taken his family for granted in the past, but now, when he thought about dying, he wanted his wife, children and mother near him. Nothing else could provide the depth of comfort.

His second answer was his friends. Todd described his thought process and how he was sure this answer could withstand the CAP test.

His third answer was books. He had chosen them after hearing his wife's conclusion, but it made sense. Books could provide information for whatever situation he was in, allow him to continue learning, and offer some recreation.

---

**What are your top three? Using the same criteria, make your own list.**

---

"These are good answers," Blake said. "Let's talk about family and friends." He asked Todd if he remembered the statement about the bottom line being less important than everyone winning.

"Yes," said Todd, "but I have to admit that I don't fully understand the concept."

"Then this could be one of the most profound conversations of your life," Blake stated simply. "I believe that relationships with people are one of the two most important things in life. If you do too, then are you treating them that way? Are you guarding and protecting the relationships you have with your friends and family? Are you building relationships in your life? We define building relationships as pursuing, pleasing and meeting the needs of the people around you. At Severson Systems, we are intentional about pursuing, pleasing and meeting the needs of everyone we do business with, including our employees, friends and family. It's the benchmark of our success."

"I've seen that already in my business dealings with you," agreed Todd. "It's what interested me to the point that I am sitting here today."

"It is intriguing. You see, there is no such entity as 'the business' or 'the company'—both are defined by the people in the business or company. People do business with people. Every single thing we do in life revolves around our interaction with others. And success in your life depends on this. You said it your-self—that people and personal relationships are the most impor-tant things in your life. If you consciously understand this and make it the goal of your life to build relationships by seeking to pursue, please and meet their needs, you will be successful. I can't stress this enough."

Blake shifted forward in his seat. "Todd, most people focus on the left side of the equation. They are more interested in their goals to acquire and achieve than they are interested in how they interact with the people in the process. In fact, this is my impres-sion of you, Todd. You have become relationally unconscious. When you interviewed with us, it was all about what you had acquired and achieved in your life, not about the people in your life. It felt like you only had people in your life to show what you had done for yourself. I don't believe you will become truly happy until you figure out how to change your focus to the *Right Side of the Equation*. When you focus on how people interact to achieve the left side, things will change."

Todd was stunned. Nobody had ever given him feedback that was this direct and biting. Todd's mind drifted for a moment as he pondered what he heard. He knew it was true, but it didn't feel good.

"This change in focus requires some changes in everyday thinking. You need to become the same person 24 hours a day. You need to treat others in ways that demonstrate you are pur-suing them, pleasing them and meeting their needs—something few people do. You need to stop excusing negative, hostile, or marginally ethical actions with the phrase 'that's business' or 'I have to look out for number one.' Reject the concept that it is okay to do something professionally that you'd never do in your personal life. There should be absolutely no difference between how you act at the office and how you act at home. You should treat your co-workers, customers, and vendors exactly the same way you treat your friends and family. We must not have one standard for how we operate at home and a different one for the office. Yet, that seems common in much of the world right now.

"That kind of behavior doesn't build relationships. It's dishonest. It lacks integrity. People take advantage of others, trying to get ahead at other people's expense. Todd, when you pursue, seek to please and meet the needs of your family, friends, employees, customers, and vendors you are building relationships. If you're not doing this, then you're tearing them down. Life doesn't have a neutral position. Anytime people think they're in neutral, they start thinking negatively. As long as you actively pursue, please and meet needs, there is no mixed message. When we get to the third step in the program you will learn how to focus on the *Right Side of the Equation* in everything you do. That's when things will change in your life."

---

***Who are you pursuing, pleasing and meeting the needs of?***

---

## TODD'S OTHER ANSWER

"Now," Blake continued, "I want to discuss your third most important value—books." Blake didn't disagree with Todd, but suggested a slight change to a broader category. "Perhaps by books, you really mean intellectual stimulation. If so, then you've come up with the same answers that nearly everyone comes to. In fact, your answers and my answers are similar."

Blake explained that the second most important thing in his life was personal relationships, combining family and friends into a single category. Third was intellectual stimulation, keeping his mind busy and fed. "Our brain thinks every waking moment. We can't stop it. It needs to be fed with information constantly. I believe we should consciously choose positive input that pushes us intellectually. Unfortunately, there is a lot of garbage out there to choose from as well."

Todd nodded in agreement.

"Todd, I'm not sure you realize the importance of the process you've just gone through. You've been forced to stop and consider what matters the most to you in life—the things you can't live without. When you did this, you determined your purpose for using the program. Now, what are you going to do with what you've discovered?"

Todd grinned sheepishly as he caught on. "I need to spend my time pursuing them."

"What if you built your life around these things?" Blake challenged. "What if you became deliberate about making sure everything you did fed this purpose? What if every decision you made was based on how well it supported the most important things in your life? And what if there was a way you could keep these things at the forefront of your mind? I can tell you with conviction that your life would change for the better. It would be more fulfilling. It would bring you true happiness. Your life would provide everlasting value."

Blake leaned back in his chair and caught his breath after his impassioned speech. Todd took a breath and leaned back too.

"Todd, if you are continually feeding your brain's desire to learn, if you are building your personal relationships, and you're living by the rules we all want in our lives, you can't help but be fulfilled," Blake summarized.

Todd was pleased that he had come up with the "right" answers. Then he realized that his three answers matched only two of Blake's answers. Blake had combined friends and family as his second choice, with intellectual stimulation as number three.

"But what was your first choice?" Todd asked.

"Oh, the first thing on my list is my faith," Blake stated with conviction. "Faith, too, shows up on almost everyone's list in some way. Maybe it's hope, purpose or God. Even though it may be a personal issue to most people, it shows up here at Severson in our rules," Blake smiled. "For now, I want you to concentrate on how the other two principles affect your life and the lives of every employee here at Severson. First, we have based our business on building strong personal relationships with each other, our customers, and our vendors by seeking to pursue them, please them and meet their needs. If this is your personal goal, then it is exactly the same as the company's. As you go about each day trying to build relationships with customers and vendors, you will be serving one of three things most important to you and helping the company at the same time. We wish more companies would figure it out. It's such a simple equation. But it's difficult to live out, which is why most people don't do it. They simply don't know how. Our program shows you how.

"The second important thing is intellectual stimulation. I work hard to keep new challenges in front of everyone here, from the guy who sweeps the floor to my top vice presidents. When I challenge people with new ideas, new programs and new goals to achieve, I am meeting one of their most important needs. In the third step of our program you will see exactly how both intellectual stimulation and relationships are at the heart of every one of our staff meetings and One-on-One meetings. But remember, the most important part is the focus on the relationships. Unfortunately, in other companies it's neglected the most.

"Now let's go back to those two dilemmas I had years ago, employees leaving and me wondering why I was here. I said the answers were the same but didn't want to elaborate on them until you had a chance to determine what was important in your life. Now let's take a look at them. The top three things the employees want to be really motivated and happy in their jobs are:

1   Enjoy the people they work with.

2   Use their skill and talent to create
    something for the company.

3   Rules

The top three things on almost everyone's list of the most important things in life are:

1   Faith

2   Relationships

3   Intellectual Stimulation

Enjoying the people you work with is entirely about relationships. Using your skill and talent to fulfill the contract is entirely about intellectual stimulation. And the rules in our lives are primarily based on Judeo-Christian values dating back to the beginning of recorded time. The rules of our lives are faith-based. Do you see how the answers to both dilemmas converged?" Blake asked.

"Well, I'll be darned—I see it!" Todd mused.

"The Program became the vehicle that helps us incorporate the three most important things in our personal lives and our professional lives and live them out on a daily basis with our employees, our families, our customers, vendors and friends."

Blake reached over and grabbed Todd's arm firmly to get his total attention. "Living life with a meaningful purpose is really life changing."

Todd nodded, still deep in his own thoughts. This was life changing. And it all made sense. That was the best part.

"Todd, now that you understand why the program exists, there's one more thing I want to go over with you before I teach you the three steps of the program. At our next meeting I'm going to go over the rules we live by, which are foundational to the program." Blake saw Todd to the door and they arranged to meet later that week.

## CHAPTER SUMMARY

- People want something more
  than the obvious.
    - Customers want more than a product.
    - Employees want more than a paycheck.
    - Married couples want more
      than roommates.
    - Kids want more than a roof over
      their heads and food on the table.
    - Friends and family want more
      than just your presence.

- The *Right Side of the Equation* helps
  us determine what people want
  and how to meet their needs.

- When we stop thinking about the wants
  and needs of the people around us, we
  become relationally unconscious.

- Relational Intelligence is when we
  continually strive to understand and meet
  the needs of the people around us.

- When we are relationally intelligent, people
  around us will help meet our own needs.

**POINTS TO PONDER**

- Do you want more than just a paycheck at work?

- Do you want something more from your marriage?

- Do you want a deeper relationship with your kids?

- Would you say you are relationally unconscious or relationally intelligent?

  — If the latter, what are you doing on a daily basis to prove it?

# 7

# Rules—A Vital Key

**B**LAKE AND TODD MET LATER THAT WEEK. "Now that we've discussed the program and its purpose, I want to talk to you about the rules," Blake began. "My experience is that most people follow a very loose set of rules, often making them up as they go or adapting them to the situation. But even though most don't live by a set of absolutes, they expect others to. Let me prove this to you. You expect that people will be 100% honest with you but I'll bet that you are not 100% honest. If you're like most people, you may tell them what you think they want to hear, even if it's not entirely accurate. Am I right?" Blake challenged.

Todd somewhat agreed. He wasn't willing to admit that Blake was right, but instantly many memories of this very thing came to mind.

"Here at Severson Systems, we believe you need to follow an absolute set of rules, both in business and your personal life. We've learned that our rules are an important component of Relational Intelligence. To be effective in a relationship, we must follow the same rules. I can tell you that our standards are pretty high, but I know they are what you want in your own life. I use a simple little exercise to determine this.

"If you were to move to a new town, what characteristics and attributes would you look for in your new circle of friends? Make a quick list of the 10–15 attributes that come to mind."

Todd started writing a list as he spoke to Blake.

1   Honest

2   Authentic

3   Moral

4   Giving

5   Caring

6   Sincere

7   Helpful

8   Positive

9   Fun

10   Respectful

11   Empathetic

12   Integrity

13   Dependable

14   Available

15   Have priorities straight

Blake looked over the list and smiled. "Todd, this list is almost identical to the list we use here at Severson Systems. I've asked this question of every employee here and have kept a running list of the answers. I have about 25 different terms. These are the criteria that folks use for choosing their friends. It's the rules they want to live by. Isn't it interesting that everyone here has the same general criteria? This means that we all should be able to get along. The only missing component, of course, is chemistry.

"We deploy these rules on a regular basis through a program we found on the web from the Ethical Practices Institute. They use ten basic principles to teach rules and as we compared the rules we chose to live by at Severson, we found that every single one correlated to one of their ten.

"The ten principles from the Ethical Practices Institute are:

1    Priorities

2    Accurate Representations

3    Integrity with civility

4    Balance

5    Leadership/Teamwork

6    Respect

7    Self Control

8    Prosperity

9    Honesty

10   Contentment

"I can tell you that every problem you've had in your life was a violation of one of these principles. Conversely, when you live by these principles, I think you'll find things go pretty well. Life gets simpler. As a company, we want to live by the same attributes and high standards that we want as individuals.

"Todd, the rules we live by play a very important role in what's important to us in life. You stated that family and friends were two of three most important things in your life. We expect that our family and friends will live by the same set of rules we developed. Unfortunately very few have a written list of these rules nor do they discuss them unless they're violated. When you have them printed, see them regularly and discuss them, they become easier to live by. That's why we post them on our desks, in the bathrooms and on the walls in our conference rooms." Blake handed the table tent from his own desk with the Severson rules printed on them.

**In every decision I make, I will strive to be...**

| | | |
|---|---|---|
| Honest | Trustworthy | Unselfish |
| Loyal | Forgiving | Visionary |
| Considerate | Positive | Intelligent |
| Authentic | Moral | Appreciative |
| Reliable | Caring/Kind | Even Tempered |
| Responsible | Fun | |

**SEVERSON SYSTEMS**

These are the rules that Severson Systems and I live by!

"We want everyone we work with to know we live by these rules and invite them to hold us accountable to them. As you'll see in step three of our program, we discuss them on a regular basis to ensure we know what they mean and how we live up to them."

Todd understood how having the rules stated, posted and discussed would make a difference. It was simple and made sense. More pieces to the puzzle fell into place.

Blake continued. "Since we are deliberate and passionate about the program, I want to make sure you understand these 'rules of conduct.' Let's spend some time going over these behaviors to be sure we know exactly what they mean to each of us. Severson employees know these rules in detail and refer to them regularly. I can tell you from experience that it's delightful to work at a place where everyone understands the rules and their meaning. It's so simple, yet no company I've encountered has defined their rules and incorporated them into their daily activity the way we have.

"This practice has another benefit. It allows us to deploy our policy manual on a regular basis. This may not sound like much, but it's very significant. We use a large national labor law firm to counsel us and to ensure we are in accordance with the law. When they saw the rules and how we deployed them they became very interested. Our attorney, Larry Sebastian, told us that employers repeatedly have the same problem when an employee brings a suit against them. The first question asked by a plaintiff's attorney is, 'Is there a policy in place?' Let's say the issue is sexual harassment. Every employer would answer in the affirmative. The next question would be, 'How do you deploy this policy?' If we were asked that question, we would state that we do have a policy and that it's deployed through our bi-weekly training program. We discuss the rules of our company and encompass every item in our policy manual, including sexual harassment. We show the training dates, the participants and the topics discussed. We have a plan that allows an employee to express a concern over any policy, state or federal law, or moral issue in an anonymous manner. One attorney told us that this program might be the only logical defense an employer has."

Todd was impressed. And, once again, the time had flown by. As Todd left, Blake encouraged him to go home and introduce the rules to his family. "Run them through the same drill, and see if they come up with the same answers. After all, the same rules apply in your home," Blake asserted.

This was an unusual concept. The rules are no different in your home. The more Todd thought about it, the more he realized it was true. If his family lived up to the rules, they would logically get along better. It did have something to do with Relational Intelligence as Blake had stated. As he sat in his office, Todd studied the table tent printed with the rules for the company. With some simple changes in terms, he could present the exact same rules to his family.

## HOMEWORK: PRACTICE THE RULES

That evening, Todd posed the question to his family about the criteria for choosing friends in a new location. They quickly jumped to the conclusion that Todd was being transferred and began offering reasons why they couldn't possibly move. Only when Todd guaranteed that this was a hypothetical exercise could they calm down enough to answer the question.

Sure enough, they came up with about 90% of the same list as he. When he brought up the ten percent that was missing, they agreed these descriptive terms should be added. Like magic, they had exactly the same list he and Blake had developed.

Todd presented the laminated cards they used at the company, and then made similar ones for each of them the following day. Todd was anxious to see what kind of impact these written rules might have on the Hanson household.

The following Friday, Todd shared with Blake how the "rules" evening had gone. He mentioned he created his own family cards at the local print shop and placed them around the house. Blake was very pleased with how far Todd had taken their lesson. He went out of his way to call in a few of the other company vice presidents and praised what he had done. They had a simple celebration, which really made an impression on Todd. He walked on air for the next three days.

**CHAPTER SUMMARY**

- There are rules in society that we expect each other to abide by.

- Often we expect others to follow the rules to a greater extent than we do ourselves.

- The ten basic rules we all want to live by are:
  — Priorities
  — Accurate Representations
  — Integrity and Civility
  — Balance
  — Leadership/Teamwork
  — Respect
  — Self-control
  — Prosperity
  — Honesty
  — Contentment

- Your rules have a direct correlation to your company policies. This program will help you deploy your company policies on a regular basis.

- Developing and living up to rules in your life is a component of your Relational Intelligence.

- It's not difficult to make a list of the rules you want in your life and to post that list in frequented areas.

## Points to Ponder

- What rules do you expect people around you to follow?
  - — Do you follow the same set of rules?
  - — Who holds you accountable to following those rules?
  - — Are your rules absolute or relative to the situation?
  - — Do you need to follow the rules only a little better than the next person?
  - — How might people behave around you if you raised the bar and followed absolute rules?

# 8

# Step One—
# Goals and Objectives

## THE LEFT SIDE OF THE EQUATION

"ODD, NOW THAT YOU UNDERSTAND why we started this program and the rules we follow, our next step is to actually teach you the program. Step one is about establishing the goals and objectives we want to accomplish," Blake instructed. "Do you have a written set of goals for what you want to accomplish next year?"

Todd reluctantly shook his head and said, "No," but said that he did have ideas and goals in his head.

"Don't worry," Blake responded. "Only 3% of the population have written goals and less than 1% update their goals on a regular basis. I've done some research on why people don't do this. I think it was Brian Tracy who gave four very succinct reasons:

1   They aren't serious about their goals

2   They don't understand the importance of setting goals

3   Fear of rejection from criticism of possible goals

4   Fear of failure

"Here's the problem. Without written goals, our wants and needs change too often, for many that means daily. If our wants and needs change daily, it will be impossible for anyone around us to help us meet our goals. Remember, in every case people are required to help us meet our needs. Let's say, for example, that a goal you set requires only your involvement. If you set one goal in your head today and then wake up tomorrow without completing it, you will be disappointed. Setting goals allows you and those around you to know where you are headed. Imagine a company that doesn't have goals. Without goals, we wouldn't know if we even needed to hire or fire someone. It begins to get absurd. Yet many companies don't set clearly defined goals and objectives and therefore they can't convey to their employees what needs to be done. Unless employees can fulfill their number two desire in the workplace, to fulfill the contract by creating something using their time, talent and expertise, (intellectual stimulation), they won't be happy in their job. This may cause frustration and prevent enjoying their co-workers. If that happens, a pleasant work environment will move in the opposite direction.

"I've witnessed this firsthand," remembered Todd.

"We all have. So, we set very specific goals and objectives so we know exactly what we are trying to accomplish, who we need and what they need to do to fulfill the contract. We set two kinds of goals—our Qualitative Goals and our Quantitative Goals. The Qualitative Goals present a quality statement about how we want to do business. The Quantitative Goals describe exactly what we hope to accomplish in a certain time frame. Here are our Qualitative Goals."

## Corporate Qualitative Objectives

*Customer Satisfaction*

1. People are pleased to do business with us.

*Finance*

2. We make a profit which will provide a reasonable return to our owners and investors and a reasonable wage to our employees.

*Growth*

3. We are a growing company.

*Staff Development*

4. Every person in the company continually demonstrates a desire to grow.

*Quality / Community*

5. We build high quality products that provide a value to our customers and our community.

"You can see there are five quality statements we strive to respond to—customer satisfaction, finance, growth, staff development, and quality or community."

"Looks pretty straight forward," commented Todd.

"Then we have our Quantitative Goals," Blake remarked as he handed him a second card.

## Corporate Quantitative Objectives

*Annual Sales*

1. $168 million in annual sales.

*Annual Profit*

2. 11% net profit before taxes.

*Growth*

3. A 5% growth rate in our number of customers and employees resulting in a 12% increase in sales.

*Staff Development*

4. A backup for every employee and three names from each employee.

*Quality / Community*

5. Less than 1% return rate; 100% customer satisfaction; and a 2.5% corporate giving program.

"As you can see with our quantitative goals, we also have five over-arching goals: annual sales, annual profit, growth, staff development, and quality/community.

"Todd, one of the key components to our goal setting is that they are fairly simple to remember so that each person in the company can instantly repeat them if asked. When you get an entire company focused on one set of goals and then get each person to understand their contribution toward those goals, you have a pretty good chance of succeeding. You will see in the people side of the equation how important these goals are in helping each and every person become a contributing member."

## Setting Individual Goals

"As you might have guessed, it will be very important for you to set your individual goals as they relate to the company's corporate goals. It's essentially your contribution that will help us achieve our corporate goal. What are the four or five things you need to accomplish this year so the company can reach its goals? As a regional sales manager, you play a very important role in the overall sales of the company. Your region represents 14% of the overall sales of the company, so it should be fairly easy for you to determine your number one goal. I want you to develop your top four to five goals over the next few days as part one of your homework assignments."

"Done," promised Todd.

"For part two of your homework assignments, I want you to determine the goals and objectives for your family for the next year. I know you said you have ideas of what you'd like to accomplish in your head, but I think it will be very important for them to be written down. I also want you to follow the same methods we use here at the office. Create one set of goals that are qualitative and another set that are quantitative. For example, you might come up with qualitative goals for your family that look something like this:

1   Attend church regularly

2   A growing and thriving marriage

3   Great relationship with our children/them with us

4   Financially smart

5   Contributing members of our
    neighborhood and community

Then you might develop quantitative goals that look like this:

1  Go to church twice a month

2  Meet my spouse's top ten needs

3  Meet my children's top ten needs

4  No debt except for house and 17% of our income into savings/retirement

5  Attend neighborhood clean-up and Rotary twice a month

"Todd, when families have written goals like this, things run differently. You told me your folks divorced when you were in junior high. What do you think would've happened if they had these exact set of goals in writing and did their best to achieve them? There is a good chance they may not have gotten a divorce because they focused on meeting each other's needs. I will explain what I mean by the top ten needs of your spouse and children in step two and it will make more sense. But for now, go home and develop a set of written goals for you and your family and then a set of written goals for your job," Blake encouraged Todd as he escorted him to the door.

## Todd's Family Sets Personal Goals

Todd went home and called for another family dinner night. At dinner he explained what he had learned and that he wanted them to develop as a family a set of goals for the year. What did they want to accomplish that year in terms of their marriage and with the kids? Todd's family initially thought it was a waste of time, but Todd brought up Blake's comment about his parents and how they may not have gotten a divorce when he was a kid if they had set goals annually. The family agreed and spent some time talking about their goals. Todd and Sarah set as one of their goals to grow closer to each other in their marriage. They set a goal to be better parents, even though none of them could define what that might look like. They also set some financial goals and a goal to take at least three family vacations that year.

**CHAPTER SUMMARY**

- Approximately 3% of the population has written goals.
- Approximately 1% update those goals on a regular basis.
- We need both qualitative goals and quantitative goals.
- You need goals in all aspects of your life:
  — Personal
  — Work
  — Family

## POINTS TO PONDER

- Do you have written goals?
  — If not, why not?
  — What has prevented you
    from writing your goals?

- What are your qualitative goals (how
  you want things to turn out)?

- What are your quantitative goals
  (the specific outcome)?

- Will you make a list of your qualitative and
  quantitative goals today in all aspects of
  your life—personal, work and family?

# 9

# Step Two— Team Performance

## THE RIGHT SIDE OF THE EQUATION

THE NEXT WEEK, Todd arrived at Blake's office at his normal time ready to learn the next step in the program. "Come on in," Blake offered with a big smile as Todd entered his office. "I can't wait to tell you about The *Right Side of the Equation*, but first, how did you do on your company goals and then how did things go with your family?"

"It went well on both assignments. I spent some time looking over our corporate goals and then pondered what my personal contribution to those goals might be."

Todd handed Blake a piece of paper with his goals:

1  $24 million in sales for the region

2  $2.4 million in net profit from the region

3  15 new customers (15% growth for region)

4  Fully trained backup for each member
   of my team (including me)

5  100% customer satisfaction (with 1% return rate)

He explained, "My region represents 14% of the company's revenue. I looked at our corporate quantitative goals and figured out what 14% of those goals were."

This was very good. Blake was pleased with Todd. He got it.

"Superb job, Todd!" Blake exclaimed. "We will talk about your goals in a few minutes when we get into Step Two of the program. Now that you understand Step One, the next thing we are going to do is understand the dynamics of how people play into those goals and objectives. We can't possibly reach our goals without people. But we've learned that we have a much better chance of meeting them if we understand our employees' goals, too. We know that people want to enjoy the people they work with, they want to fulfill the contract by using their skills and talents to accomplish something for the company, they want rules and they want to be recognized for the work they complete.

"Let's talk just for a moment about enjoying the people you work with. Remember we talked about the Five Cs we look for in people: Character, Competency, Chemistry, Contribution and Capability? These play a major part in enjoying who you work with and are a major component of Relational Intelligence. We try to find people who appear to have these attributes, but it's hard to really know someone before you hire them. We know that we can further develop these attributes once they become an employee. Getting people to enjoy who they work with mostly depends on the third step in our program. But it can't happen without the first and the second step, too. Unless we have clearly defined goals and jobs, it is unclear what they need to accomplish to please their employer. In Step Two I will show you how we make people successful in their positions. Then in Step Three, I'll show you how we interact with each other in a way that ultimately leads to job success and relational contentment."

## DEFINE JOBS

"First we need to make sure we have the right people in the right positions. In Jim Collins' book, *Good To Great*, he called this, 'having the right people in the right seat on the bus.' To determine this, I ask two very simple questions:

1   Can you support and defend why
    each person is on your team?

2   Are they more valuable to you here or would you
    rather have them working for your competitor?

Let's take the first question. Your answer should be you couldn't meet your annual goals without him or her on your team. They possess the Five Cs, meaning they compliment the other members of your team and are making important contributions. Too many times, someone ends up on a team then after awhile nobody can remember why. Many of the Five Cs have either faded away or are gone all together. On a regular basis, I will ask you to support and defend your team members. You need to have a good answer to these questions," Blake warned.

"Now let's take the second question. The simplest test we've developed for determining whether someone should move on is, 'Would I want him or her working for my competitor?' Would it be detrimental to our company if he were on our competitor's team? Often we have employees that seem to be lacking in one or more areas of the Five Cs and we can't seem to coach them out of it. Simply ask the question, 'Do I want them working for my competitor?'

"As a part of the drill of answering these two questions, you must determine what each person does to be a contributing, imperative member of your team. You must look at each person's individual goals, make sure they are in sync with the corporate goals and that they can and will be achieved. We want to complete this picture." Blake handed Todd this diagram:

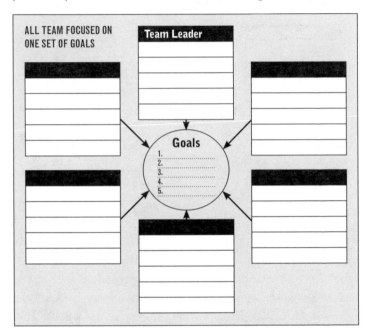

"If you have five people on your team, you might have a chart that looks like this. If each person listed their top four to five goals and each of those goals were designed to support the division's goals, which in turn support the corporate goals, then we have a fighting chance of meeting annual corporate objectives. So this might be a chart of your division. In the center we could list the goals you gave me a few minutes ago. Then each of the people on your team might list their individual goals that would be required to meet those divisional goals. Similarly, I have a diagram with all of my direct reports. It looks like this," he offered as he handed him the chart.

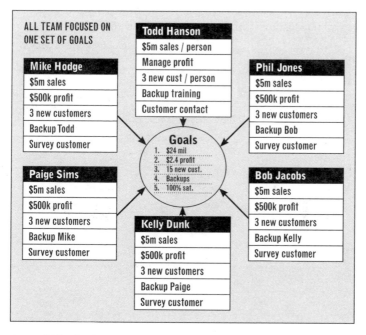

As Todd looked it over, Blake continued.

"It's really a corporate organizational chart which adds the goals for each person beneath their name. This is very important. Every department creates this chart so we have a pyramid of charts, each supporting the individual division goals. These charts collectively support the goals of the organization. We can support and defend why each employee is on their divisional team and how his or her contribution supports the whole. Our experience has been that when every person knows their individual goals and how they play into the organizational goals, we almost always reach our corporate goals."

## CHAPTER SUMMARY

- Individual jobs should be very well defined.

- You must be able to support and defend why each person is on your team.

  — A key question is, "Would I want them playing for my competitor?"

- Each department in your company should have a chart showing their departmental goals and the individual goals of each person.

## POINTS TO PONDER

- Can you support and defend each person on your team?

- Would you rather have someone on your team working for your competitor?

# 10

# The Five Cs

"**B**EFORE WE GO ANY FURTHER, I want to spend a few minutes in more detail discussing the Five Cs," Blake told Todd. "You need to use them when evaluating your team and when interviewing any potential new hires. The better you get at detecting where people stand relating to the Five Cs, the more you will master Relational Intelligence."

## CHARACTER

"First, let's talk about Character. For us, a person's character is determined by how well they live out our rules and ethics program. Now, people tend to set their own relative bar for morality; seldom do they use an absolute bar. The absolute bar means there is one standard that is immovable. The relative bar allows a person to adjust their standard based on the current situation or collective society. Most people use relative rules and ethics.

"Here at Severson, we strive for the absolute rules and ethics. It's very difficult. We all make mistakes on a regular basis. But we strive for it because those we do business with expect nothing less. Everyone we do business with wants us to live up to those rules and ethics we have in place. When we don't, they lose trust and that will affect their decision to do business with us. However, this also is relative. Though people expect us to be ethical, they are surprised when we are—because society has allowed us to break rules as a common practice. We want to raise the bar back up to the absolute level for two reasons: it's the right thing to do and it will set us apart from everyone else," Blake explained.

Todd interjected, "I'm not completely sure about absolute and relative rules—could you explain that a bit more?"

"Sure. Let's see, if we were to take honesty as the rule we were evaluating, we could measure whether a person was 100% honest in every situation or if they were mostly honest or only somewhat honest. If we were to ask the average person if they were honest, they would likely say "yes" and it would be a relative answer. They would do a quick evaluation and determine that compared to most people, they were honest. But if we pressed a little harder we could find out if they were absolutely honest or relatively honest. We could ask them if they ever embellish or withhold information. Do they ever round up numbers or add a little extra information in stories to make them sound better? Do they report 100% of their income or try to squeeze in a few questionable deductions? Do they always tell their boss the truth or do they withhold information? How about in a sales situation—is everything disclosed when a person asks a specific question? Do they tell what they would consider a white lie, meaning it was a clean lie because no one would be hurt by it?

"For those we're around a lot, we can watch, listen and know whether they're honest or not. If we can't gain personal experience, then we have to either ask people close to them or ask them questions that might help us determine their character. We encourage our employees to do their best to live up to our rules and ethics. We want to do our best to find prospective employees who desire to strive for the absolute bar. We want to do our best to live up to the standards we have set," Blake clarified.

"So Todd, when you interview someone, there are two questions to ask. First, do they believe that for us to be successful in business we need to be slightly more honest than our competitors, i.e., the relative bar, or do we need to strive for the absolute bar? Second, when you show them our rules and ethics program, do they have a desire to live up to those standards at the highest level? Based on past performance, would this be difficult?"

Todd shifted in his chair, character wasn't his strongest suit.

## COMPETENCY

"Next, let's talk about Competency. Competency is the sum of the pieces that comprise a person's skills. The question we're asking is, 'Does this person have the mental and physical ability and perhaps the experience necessary to do the job?' To answer this question we will look at the person's track record, education and experience then compare that to the specific requirements for the position. If there are two areas that people tend to under hire in, they're competency and capability. Many companies think if they hire the less experienced person to do the job, they can pay less and train them up into the position. It seldom works. Too much time is lost training because they're not competent.

"We've learned this the hard way. When we were young and growing, we needed a new production manager. We hired someone who scored really high in the character, chemistry, and capability areas but lacked experience and consequently was less competent. As a result, he didn't make much of a contribution and we struggled. When we recognized how important competency was and we made an investment in the right person, we were so surprised at how different things were. We thought we over-hired for the position with our next production manager who did the same thing at a much larger company. It worked. Hiring someone with more experience than we thought we needed turned out great. Part of what attracted him to the position was the growth opportunity he saw in our company. But the biggest attractor was our rules and ethics program. We are a company of integrity and that was more important to him than a firm of relative ethics," Blake explained to Todd.

"We've learned our lesson and now we only look at people who appear to be overqualified for the position and are clearly competent. Take you for example. I'm guessing you thought you could do this job in your sleep."

"That was true," Todd acknowledged.

"We did our homework. We knew exactly how much you could generate and when we moved you into your region, we nearly doubled our expectation for that region based on where we placed your competency level. We believe that competency is a significant component to being able to make a contribution. Todd, remember this, look for a person that's two levels above the position you're trying to fill. Even if it costs more," Blake advised with a strong tone.

## CHEMISTRY

"Now let's talk about Chemistry. This one is sometimes difficult when you are recruiting and interviewing people because they will naturally put their best foot forward. Often it's not until you spend more time with them that you are able to better assess the chemistry. That's why for any significant hire, we always include a lunch or dinner in the interview process. If the person is married, we do all we can to get their spouse to the lunch or dinner. We like to watch how the person interacts with his or her spouse. How do they treat them? What is their interaction like?

We glean a lot of information from that interaction. It also plays into their character. You may think that was absent from your interview process but we had already had several dinners with you and Sarah on some of our promotion trips. We already had a good feel about the chemistry component with you. But with people you meet for the first time, you need to get away from the office and spend time in the *Right Side of the Equation* to get to know them. The bottom line question we ask ourselves about any hire is, 'Can we invite them to our home for dinner, again and again, and enjoy it?' We try to form an opinion on everyone, even our part time employees. You will also see that it's listed on our scorecards. It's a really good indicator for whether we like someone or not. Remember, it's the sum of the pieces that we look for in a person, not any single attribute."

## CAPABILITY

"Next let's discuss Capability. This is the heart of the *Right Side of the Equation* and the one I believe is overlooked the most. It's often hard to diagnose. We want to find the answer to the question, 'Is there anything going on in the person's life that would prevent them from operating to the best of their ability?' Is there a major change in financial condition, like a bankruptcy? Is there a major change in their marital status or family status? Are they just coming out of rehab? We can't legally ask that question directly. What's more, the average person would answer, 'No.' Most people think they can overcome the seasons in their lives and continue to perform to the best of their ability. Statistics and experience reveal something very different. Good season or bad season, both will take a toll on performance in the workplace and in their personal life. For the new hire, we are looking for the beginning or recent end to a major event. We look for changes in family status, i.e. recent marriages or divorces, deaths or serious illnesses, recent births and even children recently leaving the house for college. Because many of these questions are personal in nature, we need to be very careful so that we don't break any laws. We can ask very simple questions about what the person does for fun and what a typical weekend over the past month looked like. If a person had a recent change in the family, that will likely come up as they describe recent weekends. Once they bring it up, you can usually ask them other related questions. For example, if the person says she usually spends weekends with her husband and children, you can ask how long they've been married and the age of the children. If you hear they've been married for two months but the kids are 12, 10, 8, 6 and 5, you know you likely have someone who was recently remarried and now has a blended family. Blending families can be very difficult in the early months and this person is likely in the midst of a season that is both good and bad. Her performance most likely won't be at its best for at least another 6–12 months. This may be okay, but we need to plan for it, know what to expect and how to help her with that process. She must, however, be an outstanding member of the team once the season is over.

"We need to recognize that when we relocate an employee for a position, their performance will not be at its peak for some time because we are putting them through a season. Starting a new job is a season unto itself. We all know there's a ramp up period. When we move entire families into a new community, we have to expect that for several months they will be going through some change that will impact their ability to function at work and at home. We need to recognize this and help people through those seasons. One of the best things we've done is to make sure we don't try to kill the person with production in the first few months. They need to be at home early and make sure their family is getting acclimated. We want to make sure they have a really good balance for the first three to six months on the job," Blake explained.

"Another good reason for the lunch or dinner is many times people will relax and start talking about what's going on in their lives. This might give us a clue as to whether they are in the midst of a season or about to go into or come out of one."

## CONTRIBUTION

"Finally, I want to talk about the final 'C'—Contribution. We can get someone who has all the character, competency, chemistry, and capability that we're looking for, but if they can't or won't make a contribution for some reason, they cannot be a viable part of our team.

"For the new hires, the contribution component has to be based on their track record. Have they already had a good scoring career? That's the question we're looking to answer. The NBA or professional baseball is a good analogy to use here. If one team is looking to pick up a free agent, they will look at most of the Five Cs and see if there's a fit with their team. For the contribution component, they look at their ability to put points on the board. In baseball they look at the batting average. In basketball they look at the scoring, rebounding and assists. Many teams will think some improvement can be done with great coaching. However, they will not take players with sub par scoring ability and hope to dramatically change them. The same is true in business. You cannot take someone who tells you they will be a big contributor to your team but has never been able to do it before. They may give you great reasons for why they couldn't do it in the past but without the track record, you shouldn't make the deal. We've learned this the hard way, too. We've had many people who pass the first four Cs with flying colors but they had a horrible scoring career. We've learned that these people are good talkers and can sell you on what they think they can do, but they've never actually done it before.

"For your existing team it's usually something different. Sometimes a person has had a good career and has been able to contribute, but is beginning to falter. When this happens it's usually one of a few things. Either he is in the midst of a season and it hasn't been recognized, or the demands of the job have changed and you've outgrown his competency level. Or perhaps the person is simply tired of pushing the performance requirements and wants to slow down. The problem with the latter is that many employees often feel entitled to remain in a position because they've done so well for so many years. They forget that they were paid the wage they agreed to for that performance and it didn't entitle them to an extended payout while they didn't do anything. Sometimes you need to put that in writing so the employee recognizes they are being paid for this month's work, not a payout over many years," Blake explained in a somewhat perturbed tone.

"Todd, the Five Cs are a really important component to success in business. They are the key to having the right person in the right position on your team so they can score the most points. Remember these when you deal with your existing team so you can diagnose problems and use them when you are evaluating someone new for your team. As usual, keep these in mind at home. You're not going to get rid of any of your family members, but you can diagnose problems that may be a result of a problem in one of the Five Cs and then help your family member work through the issues."

## Chapter Summary

- A person's character is measured by how well they live out the absolute rules of our society, not relative rules.

- Most people would say they are honest. But that might mean slightly more honest than most other people, instead of 100% honest.

- Competency is the sum of a person's skills.

- It's best to hire someone with more competency than less for a position.

  — When in doubt—over hire.

- The best test for chemistry is, "Can you invite the person over for dinner and enjoy it, again and again?"

- Capability means, "Is there anything going on in the person's life that would prevent him from accomplishing his goals?"

- If a person is going through a season, don't overload them with work. Do the opposite.

- Contribution is a person's ability to accomplish what they were hired for; I call it, "Putting points on the board."

- Beware of those who talk a good talk but have accomplished little.

**POINTS TO PONDER**

- Would you say that you are 100% honest, mostly honest or slightly honest?

- In what areas are you very competent?

- How would the people around you pass the chemistry test?

- Is there anything going on in your life that's affecting your capability on the job?

- What is your greatest contribution to your job and to your family?

# 11

# Aligning Expectations

"THE SECOND PART OF STEP TWO relates to what we expect from each other. We all have expectations, but if we don't tell each other what they are, how can anyone hope to meet them? We all have a desire to meet our employer's expectations of us. But when our employer doesn't communicate exactly what he or she would like us to accomplish, there's a good chance we will do something else. This is true in all of our relationships. We have expectations of each other and when we don't meet those expectations people become disappointed, frustrated, even infuriated. But the solution is simple. All we have to do is talk with each other to be clear about what we would like from the start. We define expectations, then check our progress continually—weekly is best—to make sure we are living up to those expectations."

"Pretty simple, isn't it?" quipped Todd.

"It is simple, Todd. I've learned that almost every time we have a conflict, it is because people thought different things would happen. They had different expectations. Then as I studied this concept, I found we have expectations about nearly everything—our marriages, children, jobs, vacations, co-workers, bosses, and incomes—almost everything we think about. This is the problem. We build up in our minds how we think something should go, and when it doesn't, we're disappointed. If disappointment becomes our standard reaction, we are on our way to a lifetime of failure followed by a tendency to retreat and become relationally unconscious.

"So let me ask you a question. Do you have a written list of the five or ten things Sarah wants from you to be her dream husband?" Blake asked.

Todd chuckled and shook his head.

"No problem—most people don't have that list. But tonight when you go home, I want you to ask your wife to write out a list of the five to ten things you could do that would make you her dream husband. Let me tell you what happened when I did this the first time. I went home one evening and asked my wife, Mary, for a list of the ten things that would make me her dream husband. Her first response was, 'What are you after?' as if I had an ulterior motive. I did have an ulterior motive. I told her that I wanted a growing and thriving marriage and I knew she had needs. Instead of me guessing at those needs, why didn't she just tell me? So she agreed and a few days later she handed me her list. I was relieved to find it didn't have anything I couldn't do. She listed things like, 'tell me you still love me; tell me I'm attractive to you; be a good provider for the family; etc.' So, for the next few weeks I did my best to incorporate some of those things into my daily activity. A few weeks later, I asked her how it was going, knowing it must be pretty good if I was incorporating the list into my daily activity. I was surprised when she appeared disappointed by my efforts. She said, 'Well, things are a little better.'

"I asked, 'What do you mean?'

"She said, 'Well you're kind of doing eight, nine and ten on the list and they are only worth about half a percent each.'

"A light bulb went on above my head. The list had priorities and the items were weighted. So I asked her to take the list back and put it in priority order and to weight it. A few days later I received the list again but in priority order with weights. The first item was worth 50% and the second was worth 40%. If I did the first two items on the list I'd be golden, I thought. So for the next few weeks I made sure to incorporate number one and number two on the list. So how do you think things went for me?"

"Much better, I suppose?" Todd guessed.

"Yes! What do you think that list is called?" Blake asked. Before Todd could answer, he responded, "'Job Description for Spouse.'

"Here's the problem. We think we know what our spouse wants from us because we've been married for so long, but we're really guessing. And because we're not mind readers, we usually guess wrong. The same thing happens at work. Our employees think they know what we want them to work on but unless we are clear, they will guess. So we need clearly defined job descriptions. The moment I recognized the list my wife gave me as a job description for spouse, I realized the same thing was true with my children and at work. They all had expectations of me and me of them. Within a week we were crafting new job descriptions in the office. Not the kind that state very high-level generalities and end up in the bottom drawer of your desk. I'm talking about a very specific list of what the person needs to do to be your dream employee. And that list must be specific, prioritized and weighted. Let me give you a real life example of what happened."

## FIRE THE ACCOUNTING DEPARTMENT

"At the time I asked my wife to give me her list, I was really struggling in the office with a few departments. I was ready to fire the entire accounting department. They just didn't get it and it seemed like they couldn't do anything right. Then I asked them to write their job descriptions using the same method I had used at home: make a list of the four to five things you do in the office daily, put it in priority order and give each item a weight. As soon as I receive the CFO's list, I instantly saw the problem. The number one priority on his list was Accounts Receivable, which he gave a weight of 40%. He reasoned that if he didn't collect the money for the company, we might not be in business long. Second on his list was Accounts Payable with a weight of 30%. He reasoned that unless he paid our vendors, we might not be in business long. Third was Purchasing Systems with a weight of 20%. He reasoned that because we had so many people with purchasing power, he needed to make sure systems were in place to make sure the purchasing was done properly and with the right constraints. Fourth was Reporting with a weight of 10%. He reasoned that he needed to provide me with reports on a regular basis so I could make decisions. When I saw the list I thought, 'No wonder I want to fire them, the list is in exactly the reverse order and with the reverse weights!' I explained to him that he needed to get me accurate reports on a timely basis so that I could make decisions. This was the most important thing to me with a 40–50% weight. My second was the purchasing system. We had many people who could buy things on behalf of the company and I wanted to make sure we had some controls in place to keep them from buying things they shouldn't. This was easily worth 30–40% to me. Third was Payables. We had always paid our vendors in a timely manner and it didn't require many hours. It was probably worth only 10% to me. The last thing on my list was the Receivables. We had contracts with everyone we sold to with very tight controls on when they paid. Everyone we sold to paid us like clockwork. It only needed to be looked at once in a while by the accounting department to make sure it was on track. Again this was only worth about 10% to me."

"That's incredible, Blake. What a difference. What happened?" asked Todd.

"When they clearly understood what I wanted, in what order and how heavily each item was weighted, they changed how they did things to meet the needs on my list. The weight told them how much importance and therefore how much time should be spent on each item and the priority told them the order to work on things. It was very simple for them to change how they worked on things and once they were delivering what I wanted, in the right order—things changed dramatically. They became one of the best performing departments here and I didn't fire one employee.

"The bottom line is that the first part of Step Two is to create job descriptions. The questions we try to answer are, 'Why are you here and what will you accomplish?' and 'What are the four or five things you need to accomplish in your position for us to know you fulfilled your end of the contract?' It's a blueprint for success. But there's a small problem. On any given day, there may be 20 or 30 things that you could work on. Unless we are clear about what we actually want you to do, you will guess and usually guess wrong. Have you ever walked by someone's desk and wondered, 'Why in the heck are they working on that?' It's because they wanted to fulfill the contract, but didn't know what to work on so they picked what is most fun or easiest for them. We shouldn't make them guess. Let's just tell them what they need to do to be successful in their position."

## THE RIGHT SIDE OF THE EQUATION FILTER

Blake handed Todd a card entitled, *Right Side of the Equation Filter.* "We've developed a tool that helps our employees figure out the importance of what they work on. Here's how it works.

**SEVERSON SYSTEMS**  THE RIGHT SIDE OF THE EQUATION FILTER

### Individual Accomplishment by Date*

| Accomplishment | Date |
|---|---|
| 1. | |
| 2. | |
| 3. | |
| 4. | |
| 5. | |

### Corporate Quantitative Objectives

| | |
|---|---|
| Annual Sales | |
| 1. | |
| Annual Profit | |
| 2. | |
| Growth | |
| 3. | |
| Staff Development | |
| 4. | |
| Quality / Community | |
| 5. | |

### Your Radar Screen

| | | | |
|---|---|---|---|
| 1. | 9. | 17. | 25. |
| 2. | 10. | 18. | 26. |
| 3. | 11. | 19. | 27. |
| 4. | 12. | 20. | 28. |
| 5. | 13. | 21. | 29. |
| 6. | 14. | 22. | 30. |
| 7. | 15. | 23. | 31. |
| 8. | 16. | 24. | 32. |

"Every week, we ask our employees to use the Filter. On the bottom of the card where it says, 'Your Radar Screen' we ask them to list everything that they could work on that particular week. Then we ask them to list in the center section their corporate goals, like the list you gave me. Then they look at everything listed and weigh them against the corporate goals. The items that should be their priorities for the week are those that directly affect the corporate goals. It's a way to make individual goals for the week that move us one step closer to our corporate objective. We've learned that using this tool focuses employees on our corporate goals regularly.

"Without this tool, employees have only a mental list of the 20 or 30 things on their plate. Typically they will choose what is fun or makes the most sense to them without regard to their corporate goals. Or, they will respond to urgent items that the boss wants done yesterday, or not as important items that were neglected too long. We fix that with the Filter. The Filter will help employees meet their second most important need—to fulfill the contract and accomplish something for the company. The Filter has allowed us to create the dream scenario for the manager. Imagine the employee who comes into your office and says, 'Boss, I've looked over all the things that are on my plate and weighed them against our corporate goals and my personal goals and I've come up with these five things I need to accomplish this week. How does this list look to you?' As a manager you can look over the list, be encouraging and get exactly what you want without dictating or being tyrannical to the employee. You might say something like, 'This is a great list. I have some additional information that will play into your job. In order to meet some pressing needs, if you move #20 up to your #2 position and move everything else down one and can do that by Friday, that would be terrific.' You've just spelled out exactly what your employee needs to do by Friday to be successful."

Todd smiled. "This is a really great stress reducer, too. No guesswork."

"I've been told the Filter is the biggest stress reducer ever created because it not only tells an employee what they need to do, but it also tells them what not to do this week. If you agree with your boss on the top five things you need to accomplish, by extension you consent that you won't be able to do anything with the lower 25 items on the radar screen. Now, you may agree that some items on the radar screen may need a small tweak so they don't turn into a big problem later. For example, you may have promised something to someone in a few weeks. You may need to call them and tell them it's still in the works but not arriving this week. Without the Filter, sometimes people stress out because they see all 20 or 30 items on the radar screen and presume they have to complete them all, but obviously can't. The boss may have the impression that the employee will complete them but didn't think through the timing and priority for delivery. Then a failure occurs. The Filter prevents that failure. Does all this make sense to you Todd?" Blake asked.

"It makes perfect sense. It's so simple," Todd responded.

"Good. We will use this in staff meetings that you and I are involved in and I expect you to use it with your team," Blake responded.

Todd agreed.

## Chapter Summary

- We have expectations for the people around us—at work and at home.

- Expectations must be communicated because nobody can read minds.

- Expectations have to be discussed on a regular basis.

  — Weekly is good.

- Since we all have needs, why not just get a list?

- Our list of expectations should be prioritized and weighted.

- We have expectations of all the relationships in our life—personal and professional.

- At any given moment, there are usually 20–30 things we could be working on.

- Without a priority system, you will choose what's more fun or interesting to you.

- The *Right Side of the Equation* Filter is a tool used to determine the priorities in your job.

  — More importantly, the Filter tells you and your boss what you won't be working on this week.

**POINTS TO PONDER**

- Do you have a list of the five or ten things your spouse, children and boss want for you to become successful in that position?

- Have you ever thought about the weight and priority of the things you work on?

- How often do you think you should update your lists?

- What's on your radar screen? (The 20–30 things you could work on).

# 12

# "What Does It Turn Into By When?"

"**O**KAY TODD, LET'S TALK FURTHER about the second part of Step Two of the program—Aligning Expectations. This next part I nicknamed, "What Does It Turn Into By When?" With the goals and the Filter at hand, the next step is to determine exactly what the accomplishment is and by what date. First we look at the entire year and then we back up until we come to today. For example, you declared your number one goal was to reach $24 million in sales this next year. If that's true, then what will you accomplish at the nine-month mark, then the six-month mark, the three-month mark, this month, this week and lastly today? We use a simple spreadsheet to track each team member's goals throughout the year." Blake handed Todd a spreadsheet titled, "Annual Team Accomplishments."

| Annual Team Accomplishments | | | | | | | | | | | | |
|---|---|---|---|---|---|---|---|---|---|---|---|---|
| Member | W1 | W2 | W3 | W4 | M1 | M2 | M3 | Q1 | Q2 | Q3 | Q4 | Year |
| 1 | | | | | | | | | | | | |
| 2 | | | | | | | | | | | | |
| 3 | | | | | | | | | | | | |
| 4 | | | | | | | | | | | | |
| 5 | | | | | | | | | | | | |
| 6 | | | | | | | | | | | | |

"I'd like you to take this card and write your name as Team Member One. Then fill in the goals you've developed in the boxes at the right for the year. Then work backwards and complete for each of your goals what the milestone would be at the intervals described. For example, if your number one goal for the year is $24 million in sales, what will you complete by the third quarter? Will it be $18 million in sales? If so, write that down. Your team is familiar with this form so you can obtain from them the information you will need to complete the form. You can complete this form and bring it back next week," Blake instructed.

"Once you've completed the Annual Team Accomplishments, then you can easily hold each person accountable to their weekly goals. In Step Three, you will be required to hold weekly One-on-One meetings with each team member. Part of that meeting is to make sure they are tracking with their annual goals. We use a card that lists a person's top 5 duties with room to record accomplishments and dates for that week." Blake handed Todd a card that looked like this:

| Job Descriptions, Accomplishments, Dates | | |
|---|---|---|
| *Job* | *Accomplishment* | *Date* |
| 1.<br>   A.<br>   B. | | |
| 2.<br>   A.<br>   B. | | |
| 3.<br>   A.<br>   B. | | |
| 4.<br>   A.<br>   B. | | |
| 5.<br>   A.<br>   B. | | |

Blake continued, "You will notice there are an A and a B after each priority. This is where you can add a little more detail to what exactly you are trying to accomplish. For example, there may be one or more components to completing a task. You will find that some tasks will have several sub-elements to them. A person can carry this card around and know exactly what they need to work on to be successful."

"Doesn't some of the staff think this is onerous?" Todd asked cautiously.

"It could be, Todd, and I agree. When I first developed this card, I was working with some of our warehouse construction workers who needed their goals laid out in four-hour increments. I handed them the card first thing in the morning and we went over what needed to be accomplished before noon. They completed their card in priority order and knew exactly what they needed to accomplish by noon and in what order. Then after lunch we went through the same process with a new card. Every day they were successful by completing what they needed to accomplish. On your staff you have people who don't want or need this kind of micromanagement. You may have people on your team who will do fine aligning their expectations with you on a weekly basis. You might have others with whom you can align expectations on a monthly basis. It all depends on the level of confidence you have that they will be able to complete the expectations in the order agreed upon and in the timeframe required without further intervention by you.

"To illustrate this, let's go back to my accounting department example we talked about earlier. Remember, the top four goals I wanted from the CFO were:

1. Reports
2. Purchasing guidelines
3. Accounts Payable
4. Accounts Receivable

I had a high degree of confidence in the CFO and asked him for a weekly accomplishment schedule. It might have looked like this." Blake filled out a card and presented it to Todd.

## Weekly Accomplishment Schedule

| Item | Accomplishment / Date |
|---|---|
| 1. Reports | Income statement / balance sheet on desk by Friday at 10:00 a.m. weekly |
| 2. Purchasing guidelines | Spending limits, negotiated contracts, p.o. system within 30 days |
| 3. Accounts payable | All vendors paid within 15 days of invoice |
| 4. Accounts receivable | 99% of customers paying within terms |

"When you meet with each team member on a regular basis and align expectations using this tool, your employee will know exactly what they need to accomplish, by when, to be successful. When they accomplish it, you will likely meet your goals. You will meet with Lance (Severson's National Sales Manager and Todd's boss) on a weekly basis and he will go over the exact same process with you. You will report to him how you are coming with your goals for that week, month, quarter, etc. I meet with Lance on a weekly basis for the same reason. Can you see how the process works throughout our entire company?"

Todd nodded and placed the card in his folder.

As he walked Todd to the door, Blake explained their next meeting would be to begin Step Three. And, as usual, Todd was to take home and apply what he had learned today. They didn't need the Filter or the Accomplishment cards, but they did need to align their expectations. Todd was to ask his wife and kids to make a list of five to ten things that would make him Sarah's dream husband and the kids' dream father. He gave Todd a good bit of advice.

"Todd, when you get the list back from your wife and kids, don't argue about it. You may think you're already doing the things on their lists, but just thank them and sleep on it. Then the next day, if you are unsure of what they want, ask for details. I can tell you from experience that I often get my wife's list and I think I'm already doing half the things on it well. Then the next day, when I ask for details of what her number one thing might look like, I get details that show me what her real expectation is and how I have missed it. The point is, don't argue about what's on the list. Simply thank them for taking the time to write the list and then seek clarification the next day. Waiting is important so that your emotions can calm down instead of escalating into an argument. Then remember that for things to get better, you have to actually do the things on those lists on a regular basis."

## HOMEWORK: RESEARCH AND MEET EXPECTATIONS

Todd went home and asked Sarah to make a list of the five to ten things that would make him her dream husband. Then he asked Anne and Scott to make a list of the five to ten things that would make him their dream dad. He also made lists for Sarah, Scott and Anne with plans to exchange lists once all were completed.

Sarah agreed and made a list of seven items. Todd looked at her list and was astonished. It seemed very simple.

## SARAH'S LIST OF EXPECTATIONS

1   Appreciate me.

2   Tell me I'm attractive to you. To feel wanted physically.

3   To feel wanted emotionally. Supporting each other.

4   Be a good father to Anne and Scott.

5   Continue to provide financially.

6   Save for our retirement.

7   Be a good friend, someone I can rely on.

Todd thanked Sarah for the list and decided to put it on the refrigerator so he would see it on a regular basis. He also wanted Scott and Anne to see the list so they knew their dad was committed to meeting Mom's needs. This idea brought a level of accountability as Scott and Anne could ask their dad on a regular basis if he was doing the things on their mom's list. Todd gave Sarah his list, which included the following items:

## TODD'S LIST OF EXPECTATIONS

1   Respect and admire me.

2   Support me in my decisions and
    ideas as best as possible.

3   Continue to provide a clean and comfortable
    home (add your touch to the house).

4   Continue to desire me intimately.

5   Get involved in some of my hobbies
    more, like golf or motorcycle riding.

6   Exercise with me so we both stay fit.

7   Engage in my conversations as I come
    home with these drills from work.

8   Maintain a desire to cook (I love it
    when you cook for me).

A few days later, Scott and Anne gave their lists to Todd. Their lists pleasantly surprised him:

## Anne's List of Expectations

1   Kind and considerate, cares about me

2   Patient, never angry

3   Really listens

4   Doesn't change his mind all the time

5   Someone I can look up to, that my friends like

6   Doesn't embarrass me in front of my friends

7   Treats me like a grown-up, let's me try things

8   Helps when I need help, but *doesn't* take over

9   Does fun things with me—*doesn't* try to
    make me like all the things he likes

Scott's list had the requested ten items, roughly the same as Anne's. It didn't mention "kindness" but it included a red sports car and a motorcycle.

Todd's biggest surprise was that each of them wanted to spend time with him. He thanked them for putting up with the drill, and said he really wanted to try to do and be these things for them—except for the car and motorcycle. Scott would have to negotiate separately about those. They looked skeptical, but hoped he would follow through. He hung their lists up on the refrigerator next to Sarah's.

Todd prepared a list for Scott and Anne.

1   Respect me as your father.

2   Do the best you can in school.

3   Understand that I want what is best
    for you when I discipline you.

4   Be active in our household
    (contribute to the workload).

5   Value family time (especially family
    dinners, vacations and holidays).

6   Agree to spend time with me each week.

Todd provided the same list for both of them but explained that he understood they would want to do different things as they spent time together.

Throughout the next week, Todd strove to accomplish at least one thing on each of their lists every day or two. He paid attention to making his efforts genuine. It was fun to see how creative he got with his responses.

After these simple exchanges, he felt that his relationships with his family were improving. Nothing dramatic, just new warmth and appreciation for each other. He was pleased he had accepted the job with Severson and learned about the *Right Side of the Equation*. Life was changing, and he was very happy with the direction. In case you hadn't noticed, Todd was improving the relationships with his wife and kids. He was beginning to move from being relationally unconscious to relationally intelligent.

The following Friday, Todd shared with Blake that he obtained lists from his family and how he had made a point of doing something from their lists on a regular basis. "The process really worked!" he had said, trying to keep surprise out of his voice. Blake was very pleased with Todd's reception to the program thus far. Now it was time for Todd to learn the most important part of the Program—Step Three—the fulfillment of the program.

**CHAPTER SUMMARY**

- Goals should be annualized.
  - Then working backwards, you can develop quarterly and monthly accomplishments.
  - From your weekly accomplishment lists you can create a daily list.
- We all have expectations of each other, including our spouse, children, extended family and our friends.
- Aligning those expectations on a regular basis is very important.

**POINTS TO PONDER**

- What will you accomplish this year?

- Do you have goals further broken down by the quarter and then month?

- Which ones will you choose to complete this week?

- Which ones won't you be completing this week?

- What intervals do you need for your priority lists? Hourly? Daily? Weekly? Monthly?

- Do you have a list of the five or ten things that would make you the dream spouse or parent from your spouse and children?

  — What do you think will happen if you obtain the list and do your best to fulfill it?

# 13

# Step Three— Living It Out

"**T**ODD, NOW THAT YOU HAVE A GOOD GRASP of the left and right sides of the equation, it's time for you to learn the most important step, Step Three—the fulfillment of the program. This is where most people and companies fall short. I think many people and many companies do a pretty good job of setting their goals and expectations. Some even have taken into account the people side of the equation. But I have yet to find any company that knows how to live it out for the next 12 months. The third step in our program is a system for living out your business plan, strategic objective or personal goals. Here at Severson Systems, we've perfected it and have lived it out for the past five years. It works. I call it 'becoming relationally intelligent,'" beamed Blake.

"There are two components to the third step:

1   The 50/50 Meeting. This is our secret weapon.

2   Our rules. How we live out the rules we've already discussed.

Before we move on, there's one prerequisite you need to understand—your role."

## WHAT'S YOUR ROLE?

"Todd, I believe that each of us is in one of three different roles throughout the day and throughout our lives:

- Mentor (leader, father, supervisor, coach, teacher)
- Peer (friend, coworker, spouse)
- Student (child, employee, volunteer)

It's important to understand the roles you are in and how others perceive you in these roles. People expect different things of us in each position.

"One role you take on during the day is that of leader. You might be a supervisor, coach, father, or mentor. The second role you take is that of a peer—a coworker or friend. The third is being a student or someone being mentored. That's the role you are in right this minute, Todd. If you think about it, you move in and out of these roles all day long. You're a father when you get home, a boss within your department, a coworker or peer during sales meetings, and a student at other times—like now. Once you identify the role you're in, then you need to understand what is expected of you in that role. What are your duties and responsibilities? Most important, what do the people you are interacting with need from you? What do they expect of you? Todd, do you have a desire to be a great parent to your kids?"

"Of course I do," Todd replied.

"Well, what does a great dad look like? What attributes does he have?"

Todd pondered this. "Well, he is a good leader. He is encouraging, fair, patient, loving, comforting when necessary, a teacher, and has good communication skills."

"Exactly right. In fact, we've worked up a list over the years of the attributes of the perfect father, adding to it from time to time. It's the same list I use for the perfect mentor, supervisor, and coach. Here's a copy. It includes the characteristics you just mentioned, and a few more. Tell me if you agree with the others."

**SEVERSON SYSTEMS**                          THE PERFECT MENTOR

| | |
|---|---|
| Honest | Communicative |
| Moral | Courageous |
| Authentic | Driven |
| High level of integrity | Patient |
| Respected | Intelligent |
| Visionary | Fair |
| Positive | Respected |
| Friendly | Caring |
| Empowering | Focused |
| Sensible | Humble |
| Comforting | Forgiving |
| Teaching | Recognizes my skills |
| Personable | Empathetic |
| Rewarding | Supportive |
| Disciplining | Strategic |
| Encouraging | Reasonable |
| Experienced | Brings out the best in me |

"Do you see anything on the list you don't agree with or would like to take off?" Blake asked.

"No, I like all these attributes," Todd told him.

"Do people think you are all of those things when you are in the role of supervisor, coach, mentor or father?"

"Probably not."

"You're probably right. But, since you have a desire to become that person, we're going to do our best to help you become that person. It's part of Step Three. Let me give you the lists we developed over the years for the Peer/Friend Role and for the role of the Student. See if you see some similarities on the pages." He handed Todd two more sheets of paper.

| SEVERSON SYSTEMS | | THE PERFECT FRIEND / PEER |
|---|---|---|
| Honest | Committed | Empathetic |
| Moral | Encouraging | Considerate |
| Authentic | Straightforward | Open |
| High level of integrity | Loyal | Shares in your pain |
| Friendly | Candid | Shares in your gains |
| Respected | A good listener | There for you |
| Responsible | Confidential | Supportive |
| Objective | Constructive | Sets a good example |
| Sincere | Caring | Non-judgmental |
| Comforting | Kind | Has similar interests |
| Accessible | Trustworthy | |

**SEVERSON**
SYSTEMS

THE PERFECT STUDENT

| | | |
|---|---|---|
| Honest | Dependable | A good listener |
| Enthusiastic | Punctual | Open minded |
| Interested | Respectful | Willing to learn |
| Authentic | Attentive | Asks good questions |
| Positive | Consistent | Does not procrastinate |
| Respected | Grateful | Non-judgmental |
| Mature | Helpful | Has good study habits |
| Courteous | Committed | |

"Todd, if you knew this is what people expected of you when you were in one of these roles, and you did your best to be that person, can you see how things might change? How would this contribute to building relationships? These characteristics and attributes are essential for people to enjoy the people they work with. Every employee here at Severson has a copy of these three lists. Part of our regular staff meetings and One-on-One meetings is to go through the lists and make sure we're living up to them. We hold each other accountable to the lists. I encourage every employee here and my family at home to tell me when I'm demonstrating something other than the characteristics on the list. Allowing others to give me this kind of feedback holds me accountable and helps me build stronger relationships. But don't worry that it might allow some people to take advantage of me. Nothing will change the fact that I am the boss here. I own the company and will remain the person who makes the final decision until I replace myself, sell the company, or die. The same thing holds true of you as a parent, coach, or mentor."

It all made sense to Todd.

### Homework: Recognize Roles

"Todd, I want you to start critiquing your role as father and supervisor, husband and friend, and as a student. Rate yourself for every attribute on the lists. Then strive to improve where you think you need improvement. We actually score each other on how well we do in each of the roles as part of our quarterly scorecards. I'll tell you more about that later."

After their meeting, Todd started observing the people in his office, noticing how they carried out their various roles. All seemed to strive to demonstrate the qualities on the three lists. What he found most intriguing were the responses and reactions they were getting from co-workers. Everyone seemed to have more respect for each other than in other companies. People were more polite and had a positive and friendly attitude.

At home that week, Todd studied the qualities of a mentor and tried to improve himself in areas where he had often failed. He'd never been very patient or encouraging with his kids. This was his biggest challenge. He made a point of giving each of them some form of support every day. He started out small, so it didn't come off as patronizing. Within a few days, Scott and Anne had a little more bounce in their step and showed him respect.

### The Secret Weapon—The 50/50 Meeting

"Okay, now that we've gone over your roles, let's talk about our secret weapon—the 50/50 Meeting. This is the most important part of the whole program. I believe that if you practice it, you will be significantly more successful in your personal and professional life. The 50/50 Meeting is a meeting in which you spend the first 50% of the meeting discussing the left side of the equation—a person's goals, objectives and what they turn into by when. In essence, it's what the person needs to do to be successful. The other 50% is spent making sure they are capable of reaching those goals, objectives and accomplishments. It's assessing whether they have something going on in their life that would prevent them from accomplishing their goals and objectives," Blake explained.

"There are two kinds of 50/50 Meetings; one is with a group and the other is a one-on-one meeting. Different things are accomplished at each meeting. The group meeting is designed to communicate with our team our personal contributions and anything that might affect the team. It's a time to get to know each other in a broad perspective. The One-on-One is designed to align personal expectations with our supervisor and inform him or her of anything that might prevent someone from accomplishing the goals. The order in which we discuss our two topics is very important. We need to discuss the goals and expectations first and then finish with what's going on in his or her life. Here's why. The first part of the meeting explains what we need to do to be successful in our role. It provides the key to meeting the second most important goal for an employee—to accomplish something for the company using their time, talent and expertise. The second half of the meeting provides the key to meeting their most important goal—enjoying the people they work with. If you first show them how to be successful and then you spend the right amount of time talking with them about whatever they want to talk about, they will leave the meeting energized. They will leave knowing, consciously or subconsciously, 'My boss told me exactly how I can be successful in my position and it appeared he was interested in me as a person.' This is very different from how I used to run things," Blake confessed.

"Remember how this program first started? I had trouble attracting and retaining employees and learned the most important thing they wanted was to enjoy the people they worked with. Well, it started with me. They didn't enjoy me. It was because I appeared to have a one-track mind, focused strictly on business. When I walked through the building, I was so focused on getting the job done; I didn't even recognize them as people. I didn't smile much, I didn't talk to them much, and I didn't do anything that recognized them as anything other than an employee who was there to get a job done. As I started to have meetings with them and actually talk to them as people, they told me more about their lives and vice versa. We started relationships that didn't exist before. I did care about them, I just didn't know how to show them I cared. My method of acting like I cared was to ask how the family was as I walked them out of my office or back to their work area. I was the boss who focused 98% on getting the job done and 2% on how they were doing as employees. If I were to pursue them, try to please them and do my best to meet their needs, I would have to spend more time with them to understand what those needs were. Boy, was I surprised at the outcome! As we developed the 50/50 Meeting, it was easier than I expected, but the most shocking thing was the result. I enjoyed my employees and they enjoyed me. When that happened, our turnover rate dropped dramatically and productivity went up. My employees didn't want to let me down by leaving or underperforming. Everything improved. And it was so simple. Over the course of the past five years, we developed and refined what has become our secret weapon, the 50/50 Meeting. In this process, we found it applies to our employees, our customers, our vendors and to the people in our personal lives," Blake shared passionately. "It's the key to Relational Intelligence. If you spend as much time truly talking with them as you do telling them what to do, you can't help but form a relationship. And you never have to discuss anything personal if they don't want to," Blake continued.

They spent a little over an hour going over the basics to the 50/50 Meetings and agreed they would start their next appointment with the Group 50/50 Meeting.

**CHAPTER SUMMARY**

- There are three roles we move in and out of each day:
  - Mentor (leader, father, supervisor, coach, teacher)
  - Peer (friend, coworker, spouse)
  - Student (child, employee, volunteer)
- The 50/50 Meeting is the key to the *Right Side of the Equation* Program
  - There are two types of 50/50 Meetings
    - Individual
    - Group
- The key to a 50/50 Meeting is to:
  - Spend the first 50% of the meeting aligning expectations.
  - Spend the second 50% of the meeting talking with the person—as a person.

## Points to Ponder

- How well do you rate yourself in each of the three roles?

- How would others rate you in those roles?

- Can you start holding 50/50 Meetings with the people around you?

# 14

# The Group
# 50/50 Meeting

"**T**ODD, LAST WEEK WE DISCUSSED just the basics of the 50/50 Meeting," Blake began at their next session. "Now I want to teach you how to accomplish them. We'll start with the group meeting. We hold staff meetings once a week here, as you know. You've experienced the 50/50 Meeting without even knowing it. We spend the first half, like most companies, going over typical staff meeting items: how are the teams doing, how are we coming on our goals, objectives, accomplishments, deadlines, problems and team scores. But then we clear the table of our agendas and work papers and go around the room to see how people are doing. In many companies this is the chatter that takes place while people are waiting for everyone to get to the meeting. Here it's the deliberate second half of our meeting. It's also when we have our rules discussions. Let me walk you through an actual meeting we held here a few summers ago.

"We began the meeting at 11:00 in the morning. There were ten of us in the room and this was a sales meeting for one of our regions. Bob Simpson, the regional manager, had eight of his salespeople in attendance who were direct reports. Bob wanted me to show him how to conduct a 50/50 Meeting, as he had not done one before. I told him to hold his staff meeting for as long as it usually took. Using his spreadsheet with individual accomplishments and dates, he went around the room and asked people to report on where they were in reaching their goals. He asked them to report any problems with orders, customer service, shipping, reporting, etc. It was a pretty standard meeting with some people achieving more than they had hoped and others achieving less. Bob did his best to ascertain why in both cases. His portion of the meeting was well run, to the point and completed in approximately 40 minutes. Then he handed it over to me and announced that I would be introducing a new portion to our meetings, which I had titled 'The 50/50 Meeting.' I had a few pizzas brought in and asked people to clear away work papers. I casually asked how everyone was doing and then, as if I was just trying to break the ice, I simply asked what people did last weekend. Little did they know it was a deliberate part of the meeting. I went around the room starting with the person on my left and asked them to tell us as much or little as they cared to about what they had done last Saturday and Sunday.

"We got half way around the room with pretty normal stuff like working in the yard, watching baseball on TV, short outings with family members, or work around the house. Then we came to Francis. She said some family members had come into town and she held an early Christmas that past weekend. It was clear she didn't want to elaborate, so we continued around the room. A few more regular weekends were shared, including one person who said he was out with his girlfriend looking at wedding rings. Everyone gave him some jabs about tying the knot. The whole process took about another 40 minutes and was quite fun. That was it. We learned what each other did on the weekend. But there were two pieces of big news that were uncovered. After the meeting was adjourned I went to Francis. I asked her what was up with the early Christmas. She said her father was dying and he wouldn't make it to Christmas, his favorite holiday, so some of her family members flew into town so they could celebrate Christmas with him for the last time. I told her I was sorry as she walked out of the room."

## A Bad Season

"I felt horrible. Francis was one of the few people in the meeting who did not make her sales goals. She had been a good employee who almost always did well. But recently she had been noticeably late on several occasions and she didn't appear to have her head in the game. Our normal method of operation would have been to tell her that we didn't know what was going on, but she needed to get to work on time and improve. Now I understood why her performance had dropped. I knew I had two choices. I could act like nothing was going on and press her to step up her performance, or I could try to help. Then a brilliant idea hit me that would turn out to be one of the keys to our success. I went to Bob, her supervisor, and asked if he had any knowledge about Francis' early Christmas. He said no, so I filled him in. He, too, felt badly, especially since he had been putting pressure on her to perform and get to work on time. I asked him what would happen if we went to two of the other sales people and asked them if they would help out, given the situation. I was sure they would. Then we could go to Francis and tell her that we wanted to give her Wednesday afternoons off so she could go sit by her father's side until he passed away or improved.

"We approached two of Bob's other salespeople from his region and told them about the early Christmas. When they heard, before we could even ask, they asked if there was anything they could do. We said yes and suggested they cover for Francis on

Wednesday afternoons. They thought it was a great idea.

"We then went to Francis and told her that Misty and Carl were going to cover for her on Wednesdays so she could leave at noon to be with her father. In tears, she said she was appreciative for the thought but didn't feel comfortable doing that. Death was scary to her and she didn't know what it would be like to sit by his side every week for a few hours. We eventually convinced her to do it," Blake beamed.

"But Todd, we didn't realize what we had done. Our culture shifted with that one event. Bob became a support to Francis, instead of an antagonist. Each week he asked her how things went with her father. Just asking the question was taking part of the burden off of Francis. Bob also wasn't so pushy when it came to her numbers. Once we found out about her situation, we knew her numbers would be off for some time. We could either support her through it or do what we had always done—tell her to 'get to work on time and keep your head in the game.' There was more that we didn't expect. She became very close friends with Carl and Misty, who were doing her job every Wednesday afternoon. Francis' father passed away within three months. A month later Francis was coming out of her deep grief. But she was a different person. She told me that Severson Systems allowed her to spend some time with her father that was perhaps the most important time in her life with him. Had he died without that time with her, she would have agonized over not spending his last days with him. In addition to that, she realized that Carl and Misty were the ones who allowed her to do this. They became very close friends and became part of her support mechanism during the last days and through the funeral services. A friendship was formed that will never be broken. In addition, several other employees brought her meals on Wednesdays to take home so she didn't have to cook for her family. The company rallied around Francis.

"What we didn't expect was who Francis became. Once she was back at work emotionally and physically, she was on fire for Severson. She almost doubled her best year's sales. She told every customer out there how great Severson was for helping her through that tough time. And she became an advocate for the firm with our employees. If anyone even started to say something negative about the company, she'd show them how and why they were wrong. We had developed a lifetime employee and all we did was treat her like we would hope to be treated under the same circumstances. It was incredible."

"That is incredible. I've never heard of anything like it," marveled Todd.

"Francis went through a season in her life. We found there are bad seasons and good seasons, both of which have the same potential impact on the company."

## A GOOD SEASON

"During that same meeting, you'll remember that one of the guys was getting picked on because he was looking at wedding rings. Well, at the time I didn't recognize it, but we were about to go through the exact same thing with him. His name was Tom. Within a year, Tom was getting ready for his wedding. And for about six weeks prior to his wedding, he became the same employee Francis was before we stepped in and helped her. Tom was regularly late for work, his sales numbers started to fall and he just wasn't into his work. It was a tension filled time for him and us. Then we realized he was going through a season just as Francis had, only it was a good season. As a result of Tom's situation, we now have a policy about weddings and seasons in general. Shortly after Tom's experience, we had another young lady, Connie, in accounting that was getting married. We went to the accounting department about two months before her wedding and asked if two or three people would not mind putting in a little extra effort on her behalf so we could give her Wednesday afternoons off to plan her wedding. They agreed and we gave her the time off. As you can imagine, a few weeks after the honeymoon was over, she was fully engaged again at work. But she was on fire for Severson exactly the same way Francis was. We allowed her to go and plan the most spectacular wedding ever.

"We could have been dense like we were with Tom and told her to get to work on time and get her head in the game. But instead, we told her to do the best she could when she was at work and instead of taking time during work to make calls about the wedding, as Tom had done, to make those calls on Wednesday afternoons. It was a simple arrangement but the outcome was far different than Tom's. We were supportive of her wedding and her head not being in the game. At the wedding, she publicly thanked her supervisor, her co-workers who did her job on Wednesdays, and Severson Systems for being 'an awesome place to work.' When Connie got back from her honeymoon, she came into my office and personally thanked me for allowing her to plan and have the best wedding she could have imagined. Her performance in accounting did something similar to Francis' in sales. She was on fire for the company and told everyone what a great place it was to work and how some of her best friends in life worked there.

"Todd, we've realized that every person is going to go through a season or two. Some will be good and some will be bad. Bad seasons are things like divorce, death, illness and bankruptcy. Good seasons are getting married, having a baby, graduating from school or moving into a house. Good or bad, they both have an effect on the person's job performance. Both can be very stressful. As a company, we have a choice. We can get angry and ignore the fact that people will undergo seasons, or we can support them. It doesn't cost us anything, but has paid huge dividends. In nearly every case the employee has been grateful to the company and his or her co-workers. We've developed a culture that is supportive of each other and have built lifetime employees who are dedicated and super-productive. It's been a major component in allowing people to enjoy those they work with.

"Oh, but there is one thing. Remember I said that nearly every employee is grateful to the company and the employees that help them through their season? Well, we've found that out of a hundred people there might be one or two who take advantage of the system. They find out we help people who are going through seasons and they somehow develop a season that lasts a lifetime. We've been able to ferret those out and move them on. In those cases, we've needed the help of our attorney so we didn't end up in a lawsuit. But it's truly a small fragment of people who have this mindset. We decided it was worth it to continue the program instead of letting one or two percent of the people spoil it for the rest.

"Todd, here are some keys to the Group 50/50 Meetings:

1   Allow people to respond to your questions
    only to the extent they feel comfortable.

2   Don't drill down if they don't want you to.

3   Don't ask personal questions.

4   Don't allow people to go too deeply in the
    group. Ask to take it offline if things get

too detailed for the group setting.

5    Make sure you cover normal staff meeting
     items first and the people side second."

## INCORPORATING THE RULES

"Todd, there is one more thing we do during the Group 50/50 Meeting, we discuss the rules we live by here at Severson. You'll remember I asked you for the rules you choose to live by and you gave me a list. Then I gave you ten overarching principles we choose to live by here at Severson. We actually discuss both lists on a regular basis. We do this so we can actively deploy our company policies and so we can agree what these rules and principles mean. I've found that if we don't do this, our morale dips. People like talking about the rules they wish to live by and how to get better. It adds a layer of accountability that everyone desires," Blake told Todd.

"There are two ways we incorporate our rules. First let's talk about the list you came up with. It's almost the same list that everyone else here came up with when they went through the same drill. You see them around the office, at workstations and in the restrooms." Blake pulled the same table tent off his desk and handed it to Todd.

**In every decision I make, I will strive to be...**

| | | |
|---|---|---|
| Honest | Trustworthy | Unselfish |
| Loyal | Forgiving | Visionary |
| Considerate | Positive | Intelligent |
| Authentic | Moral | Appreciative |
| Reliable | Caring/Kind | Even Tempered |
| Responsible | Fun | |

**SEVERSON** SYSTEMS **These are the rules that Severson Systems and I live by!**

"This is the list of rules that our employees developed that describe how we want to treat each other. But we have to discuss them on a regular basis because we might have different definitions or understandings of what each word means. Take, for example, the first word on the list, 'Honest.' Let me give you a picture of how two people could have different interpretations of honesty. When you were a kid, your mother may have told you, 'Don't play with Johnny, he's a bad apple.' Two weeks later, you call your mom on the phone and ask her if you can go to the mall with some friends. She asks who is going. You tell her, Billy, Cameron, Mike and Stu. You don't tell her that Johnny is going, too. Your reasoning is that you told the truth because the other boys were in fact going. But you told the truth with the intent to deceive. Those boys were on your mother's approved list, so of course she would allow you to go with them. Had you been fully honest and told her that Johnny was going too, she probably would not allow you to go. When you tell the truth with the intent of deceiving, it's lying and is therefore not honest.

"So in our Group 50/50 Meetings we talk about our rules. Sometimes I'll do a write-up, which I've called Value Discussions. These Value Discussions provide a common and consistent format for us to discuss issues. People here have become accustomed to hearing, 'We're going to have a Value Discussion' and they know what that means. Take, for example, 'authenticity'. It's a difficult topic to just start talking about. So I did a Value Discussion on authenticity. (Blake handed Todd the Value Discussion entitled, 'Are You Leading an Authentic Life') We talked about it throughout the company during that week's Group 50/50 Meetings. You can find a list of the Value Discussions I've written on our website. The URL is rightsideequation.com."

Todd wrote the address down.

## SEVERSON SYSTEMS

### ARE YOU LEADING AN AUTHENTIC LIFE?
*If not, you're a phony & a fraud!*

Are you living an Authentic Life? If you're not, will you really be satisfied if you stop to examine your life? So many times, people try to be something they aren't, trying to impress others or to be in a place they don't belong. If you're not living an Authentic Life, you're a phony. Eventually, this will catch up to you, and you will experience guilt, depression, and anxiety. Start taking the steps today to be 100% authentic. It builds lasting relationships, trust, and an inner peace that will put you on a path to happiness instead of disappointment.

| Your life is authentic if you... | You may be a phony if you... |
| --- | --- |
| Tell it exactly like it is. Tell the truth. | Embellish, exaggerate or flat-out lie. |
| Allow no one to feel inferior due to your perceived wealth, intellect, or accomplishments. | Flaunt what you believe to be wealth, intellect or accomplishments. |
| Accept the positive in everyone you meet and consider them no better nor worse than yourself. | Think you are better than others for any reason, i.e. personal wealth, intellect, or education. |
| Do what you say you will do when you say you will do it. | Don't follow through. |
| Allow people to accept you for who you are. | Hope to impress people with what you have or what you have done. |
| Live within your means, debt free. | Overspend or have what you have only because you've borrowed to get it. |
| Do things for self-improvement. | Do things to impress others. |
| Do things out of respect for what's right. | Do things based on what feels good. |
| Know exactly where you stand on issues. | Let society influence you. |

Before anyone will take us seriously or want to become our friend, we must be honest with ourselves and acquire the qualities listed in the first column. Eliminate anything in the second column that you are now doing. Then see how you have changed your own perspective as well as how others perceive you. Do this consciously for the next week!

## ETHICAL EXERCISES

"The second way that we deploy the rules is through Ethical Exercises. We get these from an organization called the Ethical Practices Institute. We've adopted their ten principles for ethical behavior, which I mentioned earlier. The rules on the table tent tell us how we should behave and the ethical principles set the boundaries for that behavior. Here's an overview of these principles." Blake hands Todd a list of the ten principles.

### The Ten Ethical Principles in Business

1. Priorities— Highest value = highest priority.

2. Representations— Look at the whole, not a distortion.

3. Integrity— Do what's right and truthful—with civility.

4. Balance— Balance your time wisely between work, family, faith, hobbies, and yourself.

5. Leadership/Teamwork— Add value to all situations and all people.

6. Respect— Recognize each person's value.

7. Self-control— Use your mind and your body appropriately.

8. Prosperity— Strive to gain on your own, not at the expense of others.

9. Honesty— Be 100% honest, not 99.9%.

10. Contentment— Understand your limitations.

© 2006 Ethical Practices Institute • 4170 Douglas Blvd. Granite Bay, CA 95746

"Every other week we focus on one of the ethical principles in our Group 50/50 Meeting. We either lead our own discussion on the principle or we use one of the ethical exercises from the Institute. Here's a copy of the first session the Institute provides so you can see what it's all about. They're available on the web at ethicalpractices.org."

## Principle One: Priorities

### Time Management

Does your employer really expect you to work an 8-hour workday?

In 2005, Salary.com surveyed corporate Human Resource managers, and found that companies assume that their employees waste 0.94 hours per day. But when the employees were surveyed, they admitted to actually wasting 2.09 hours per day. For the average worker, that adds up to $5,720 each year in wasted salary dollars. For an American workforce of 132 million people, that's $759 billion dollars a year.

So what did people claim as their top time-wasting activities?

- Surfing the Internet (personal use) = 44.7% (of the 10,044 people surveyed)
- Socializing with co-workers 23.4%
- Conducting personal business = 6.8%
- Spacing out = 3.9%
- Running errands = 3.1%
- Making personal phone calls = 2.3%
- Applying for other jobs = 1.3%
- Planning personal events = 1.0%
- Arriving late or leaving early = 1.0%

Ethical living means putting the right people and activities in the right order. We get to decide how we spend our time. We need to focus on the right people at the right time. There are all kinds of pressures and temptations to focus on the wrong people and things. There will be pressure to focus on personal things at work. There will be pressure to focus on work issues during family time. There will be pressure to pay attention to worthless things and ignore important relationships. Ethical living means using on-the-clock time for work and saving your personal business for scheduled breaks or after the workday ends.

### Tough Questions

1. Do you ever use on-the-clock time to do any of the activities listed above?
2. If you do, why?
3. Who benefits from your unethical use of on-the-clock time?
   - Who loses out?
   - How?
4. Do you struggle to balance your personal and professional responsibilities?
   - Are there reasonable ways in which our organization could be more supportive, flexible, and ethical in alleviating that pressure?
5. In what ways does wasting on-the-clock time also violate our organizational policies or the law?

Ethical Practices Institute • 4170 Douglas Blvd. • Granite Bay, CA 95746 • ethicalpractices.org

"Todd, it's important that we build into our Group 50/50 Meeting a discussion about ethics. It helps us maintain our focus on the third most important thing to employees in the workplace—rules. When we discuss ethics on a regular basis, it becomes easier to live ethically. There is another benefit. When our customers saw the table tents and realized that we were an Ethical Practices company, they asked questions. It gave our people a chance to explain and it became something that set us apart from our competition. It had the same impact when we interviewed people for jobs. Potential employees saw the cards or the ethics posters in the office and inquired about them. We became the place people wanted to work because rules and ethics were important to us," Blake told Todd.

"Well, as a matter of fact, I thought it was impressive when I saw them as I toured your facilities for the first time. It did have an impact on me," Todd told Blake.

"That's great. I always like to hear that it continues to work. Now let me get back to some final points on our rules. We didn't want to be a little more honest then our competition; we wanted an absolute bar. Everyone here wanted us to hold him or her accountable to it and vice versa. When we invited our employees, vendors and customers to hold us accountable to our rules and ethics, it built trust.

"It continues to set us apart from our competition as an employer, as a customer to our vendors and to our own customers. Todd, I really want you to take our rules and the ethics program we use here seriously. When you go home tonight, tell your family about our rules and ethics program then when you come back next week I'll teach you about the One-on-One 50/50 Meeting," Blake told Todd as he walked him to the door.

Todd went home that night and told his family about the

Group 50/50 Meeting and the company's rules and ethics program. Friday night was becoming a family night at the Hanson home. Sure, Scott and Anne went out after dinner, but they came to enjoy the time with their parents. More importantly, they liked the changes they saw in their dad.

## CHAPTER SUMMARY

- The first half of a Group 50/50 Meeting is to go over typical "staff meeting" agenda items relating to achievement of goals and objectives and stumbling blocks.

- The second half of the group meeting is to learn about each other and see how people are doing in general.

  — Become aware of what is appropriate and inappropriate to discuss in a 50/50 Meeting.

  — Take sensitive items offline.

- The goals and accomplishments must be done first.

- The people side must be done second.

- Everyone will go through seasons in their lives. Some will be good and some will be bad.

- We need to help people through the seasons in their lives.

- Watch out for the advantage-takers.

- We all want rules in the workplace.

- There are ten basic principles for ethical behavior (p. 175).

**POINTS TO PONDER**

- Do you remember going through a season in your life (good or bad)?

  — Did it affect your productivity?

- Did your employer support you through the season?

  — How would you have liked to have been supported through that season?

- What rules do you want to follow in the workplace?

- Wouldn't you want to help people around you if you knew they were going through a difficult season of their life?

# 15

# The One-On-One
# 50/50 Meeting, Part I

T HE NEXT WEEK, Todd reported to Blake's office as usual. He gave a brief download on how well his family had received the Group 50/50 Meeting and the rules. Todd ran his family through the scenario for determining the rules people want in life. His family said they wanted to follow those rules too. Todd had completed his first Group 50/50 Meeting earlier in the week and it had gone very well. Blake was pleased with the progress Todd was making. His life was changing just as other employees' had. Now it was time to learn about the One-on-Ones.

"Todd, today I'm going to teach you about the One-on-One 50/50 Meeting. I can't emphasize this enough; the 50/50 Meetings are our key to success. They are the key tool in getting employees to enjoy the people they work with—the number one thing they want in the workplace. It's also the key to mastering Relational Intelligence. You must spend a focused amount of attention on the people around you. Pursue them so you can determine their needs then do your best to meet those needs. Does that make sense?" Blake asked.

"It does," Todd responded.

"Okay, as with the Group 50/50, there are two components to the One-on-One 50/50 with an equal amount of time allocated to each component:

1  Show the employee what they need to
   do to be successful in their position.

2  Make sure they are capable of accomplishing
   what it is that will make them successful.

"Here are some important guidelines: your meeting will only be with the people that report directly to you. If any of your direct reports have people that report to them, they should be holding their own One-on-Ones. Because of the need to meet with each person who directly reports to you weekly, the absolute maximum number of people who directly report to you should be no greater than 30. Ideally, the number of direct reports to any one person should be 12 or less. You should hold your One-on-Ones weekly. Bi-weekly is okay, but not as good. These meetings can be fairly prompt, lasting only 5 or ten minutes, or as long as an hour. We've found that the ideal meeting is between 20 and 30 minutes," Blake informed Todd.

"Before the meeting starts, it's really important that you remember your role. You are the coach of your employees. Imagine being the head coach of a professional basketball franchise. You coach some of the best players in the world. Your job is to take great players and make them better. Help them improve the things they are really good at and help them work through the things they aren't so good at. You must put yourself in the mindset of a coach, not a dictator. You can't dictate that your NBA all-star goes out and scores 40 points. But you can coach him into scoring more and more points per game. So your first task is to look back over your list of the attributes of a great mentor and do your best to be those things for your employee during the meeting—encouraging, teaching, good listener, available, disciplinarian when necessary, rewarding when appropriate, etc."

## WHEN AND WHERE TO HOLD THE MEETING

"Schedule your One-on-One meetings when you both can take the time and it will be uninterrupted. Pick the slowest part of the week, not 20 minutes during crunch time. Your meeting place should be where you won't be interrupted. Many people meet outside the office for coffee. Others hold them in their offices or in their normal work area but make sure they give each other full attention. The location isn't important as long as you aren't interrupted or distracted by your phone, email, pager or other people. We've even taught the 50/50 Meeting to some of the contractors while they have been working on our building. They would literally hold stand-up One-on-Ones away from the normal flow of things and said it worked great. Oh, one last thing. If your direct report is a woman, make sure you hold your One-on-One in a place that isn't intimate. Don't go to a bar after work or behind closed doors in your office. We don't want people to become unfaithful to their marriages because of these meetings. Be very cautious about this, Todd."

## SUCCESS IN YOUR POSITION
## THROUGH SETTING EXPECTATIONS

"Todd, you will remember in Step Two of the Program that everyone set personal goals and objectives with accomplishments that supported our corporate annual goals and objectives. We use the *Right Side of the Equation* Filter to decipher what things are the most important to accomplish in a certain time period.

The time period will be based on the capability of the person. In some circumstances, you may need to set goals in less then weekly increments and others more. Let me give you an example. Remember my construction friends where I had set expectations twice a day, once in the morning and once after lunch? They went over with teammates what they had to accomplish by noon and then before the end of the day. At the other extreme, we have had outside salespeople that we align expectations with monthly. It all depends on how capable they are of setting goals and objectives and then carrying them out.

"During the first several weeks of your One-on-Ones, I recommend that you have your direct reports bring their *Right Side of the Equation* Filter. Have them list all the things they have on their radar screen. Then have them walk you through the process they used to determine which tasks they want to accomplish by the next meeting—their top five in priority order and weighted. Then have them develop a specific accomplishment for each priority. Hopefully they come up with a list that makes good sense to you. If not, you'll need to help them understand which things need to be done this week for them to accomplish their goals. As a good coach, you should be encouraging them for the way they thought it through, unless they just missed it. If that is the case, I will naturally challenge you on why they are on the team.

"Todd, this is a negotiation. The most important thing is that you agree on the top four to five things you would like them to accomplish, in what order and with what weight. Equally important is what they won't be doing. If you agree on which things need to be completed, by extension you are telling them the remainder of the items on their radar screen don't have to be completed. If you are crystal clear on exactly what the accomplishment looks like by what time and date, then there's a better chance they will complete it. One of the biggest mistakes is that managers and employees only work off the list on the bottom of the Filter—the entire radar screen. That list is a recipe for failure. Because there are so many things on the list, the employee will try to do something on all of them and perhaps finish nothing. They will work through the list in the order they want or believe is best. This is often not the same order the manager expects. The employee gets stressed with too much to do yet not able to accomplish anything. The manager is stressed and disappointed because his or her expectations were not met. Everyone finishes the week feeling defeated.

"There is one compromise position to consider. It's possible that you determine the top five things to be completed during the timeframe but you also agree that certain things on the radar screen need to be touched but not completed. To show you this visually, let's take a look at a real Filter." Blake hands Todd a *Right Side of the Equation* Filter from Gwen Davis.

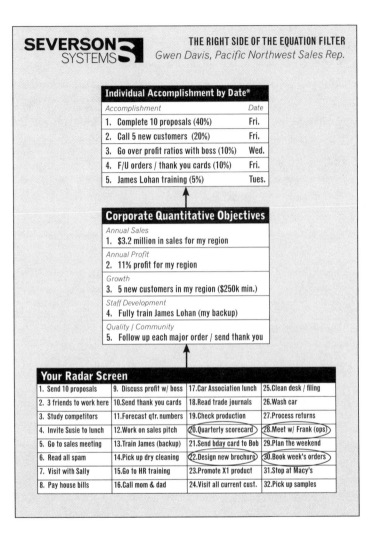

**SEVERSON** **SYSTEMS**

THE RIGHT SIDE OF THE EQUATION FILTER
*Gwen Davis, Pacific Northwest Sales Rep.*

### Individual Accomplishment by Date*

| Accomplishment | Date |
|---|---|
| 1. Complete 10 proposals (40%) | Fri. |
| 2. Call 5 new customers (20%) | Fri. |
| 3. Go over profit ratios with boss (10%) | Wed. |
| 4. F/U orders / thank you cards (10%) | Fri. |
| 5. James Lohan training (5%) | Tues. |

### Corporate Quantitative Objectives

*Annual Sales*
1. $3.2 million in sales for my region

*Annual Profit*
2. 11% profit for my region

*Growth*
3. 5 new customers in my region ($250k min.)

*Staff Development*
4. Fully train James Lohan (my backup)

*Quality / Community*
5. Follow up each major order / send thank you

### Your Radar Screen

| | | | |
|---|---|---|---|
| 1. Send 10 proposals | 9. Discuss profit w/ boss | 17. Car Association lunch | 25. Clean desk / filing |
| 2. 3 friends to work here | 10. Send thank you cards | 18. Read trade journals | 26. Wash car |
| 3. Study competitors | 11. Forecast qtr. numbers | 19. Check production | 27. Process returns |
| 4. Invite Susie to lunch | 12. Work on sales pitch | 20. Quarterly scorecard | 28. Meet w/ Frank (ops) |
| 5. Go to sales meeting | 13. Train James (backup) | 21. Send bday card to Bob | 29. Plan the weekend |
| 6. Read all spam | 14. Pick up dry cleaning | 22. Design new brochure | 30. Book week's orders |
| 7. Visit with Sally | 15. Go to HR training | 23. Promote X1 product | 31. Stop at Macy's |
| 8. Pay house bills | 16. Call mom & dad | 24. Visit all current cust. | 32. Pick up samples |

"This is from one of our salespeople. You can see that the most important thing on her list was to complete the ten proposals due that week. It was rated number one with a 40% weight so she should spend as much as 40% of her time on it. You can see items two through five and the weight of each one. You will note that the top five only add up to 85%. That's because we wanted her to spend 15% of her time doing something for each of the circled items on the radar screen so they don't become big problems by putting them off for a week or more. In many cases it's simply a phone call or email for each of the circled items to keep them active. In some cases it's following up on something that's in progress but can't be completed yet because you are waiting for someone else to deliver something," Blake explained.

"It's very important that you set realistic expectations. Be sure that the average person in the same position can accomplish the expectations you set with the same competency. Your goal is to agree upon what can be accomplished by what end date and in what order. Be specific."

## THE GRADING SYSTEM

"It's very important that you let your team know what success looks like. You need to tell them in very empirical terms. Think about it this way, when you were in school, most teachers told you what it took to get an A, B, C, D, or F. An A was 90%, B was 80% and so on. We were taught this system for at least 12 years of our life. Why did we stop? We brought that system back. We want our employees to know on a weekly basis how they are doing, so we attached a scoring system to their weekly goals. In those same studies on employee satisfaction, they found that employees wanted feedback on how they were doing on a regular basis. That's not an annual review. Some companies do their annual reviews every two or three years. Here employees know where they stand weekly. Their quarterly scores are no surprise when it comes to their goals and expectations."

"So people here know how they are doing on a weekly basis?" Todd asked.

"You bet they do. And there's a side benefit. People here can't under-perform for three weeks in a row without a corrective action plan. In fact, as you will see, supervisors never fire employees; they fire themselves. More on that in a few minutes," Blake responded.

Todd gave a surprised but affirmative nod to Blake.

"Let's go back to Gwen's expectations. It's easy to assign a scoring system to her top five goals. For her first expectation, she had to complete ten proposals that week. We could have assigned this scoring system to her number one item:

A = 10 Proposals (100%)

B = 8 Proposals (80%)

C = 7 Proposals (70%)

D = 6 Proposals (60%)

F = 5 Proposals (50%)

"With this system, it is very easy for Gwen to know where she stands. She will get strong praises if she were to come back in a week with ten or more proposals completed. She also knows in advance how we will react if she only came in with six proposals completed," Blake explained.

"What really makes this system work is that we let the employee set the expectation, the scoring system, and the consequences, and we simply provide coaching or feedback. You already know that we ask the employees to come up with their own goals and expectations. Our hope is that because of their competency levels they can develop expectations on their own that are at least 80% of what we would come up with had we dictated our expectations to them. Let me explain why this is important.

"If you grew up in California, you know that in the 4th grade you studied California missions. Often students are required to build a model of a mission as part of their curriculum. There are two ways that can happen. They can go home and tell their parents that they have to build a mission and the parent can say, 'I know exactly how we're going to do that. We're going to take sugar cubes and Elmer's glue and build this thing up.' Then the parent actually builds it. It looks great but the student is dejected because he or she really didn't build it. The parent dictated how it would be built. Conversely, the parent can encourage the student to build the mission however they want and along the way provide cursory advice on how it could look better. The student is much happier because they built it and only got coaching from someone with more experience.

"The same thing is true for employees. They want to create something for the company using the time, talent and expertise for which they were hired. So we let them create their own goals and coach them along the way to match our corporate goals. Then we ask them to tell us how it should be scored. Each week when the employee uses the Filter and develops his or her expectations for the week, we also want the scoring system. If the scoring seems a little low, we simply tell them we think they can do better and encourage them to raise their numbers to where we want them. But we do allow them to negotiate and tell us why they think it needs to be where they suggested. The bottom line is this—if they design it, there's a better chance they will achieve it. The proof is in our numbers," Blake confidently told Todd.

"We allow our employees to weigh in on what levels they must hit for bonuses, raises and promotions. When you ask an employee what score they should be hitting to simply fulfill their contract, keep their job and get paid, the number us usually pretty high, like 80% or better. They need to be doing good work which most would agree is 80%. The process is great because we never get employees asking for raises who aren't performing at very good levels. Employees know where they stand at all times because we keep track of the weekly scores and provide a cumulative score for each quarter. We add up these scores at the end of the year when annual reviews for raises and promotions take place," Blake went on.

## ACCEPTING THE CONSEQUENCES

"Not only do we want the employee to set the expectation and assess their scoring weekly, we also want them to set the consequence—even as far as firing themselves. We are very encouraging when an employee develops a good set of expectations and then reaches 80% or better for what they hoped to accomplish. But when the employee doesn't hit their expectations, we use a three-step process of increased discipline. The first time an employee doesn't make his/her numbers, we simply ask what happened that caused the failure. At the end of each One-on-One, the employee leaves with an overall score for the week and a cumulative score for the quarter and year. On any given day, the employee knows exactly where he or she stands.

"If Jack Welch from GE had used this system, he would have never had to put his manager through the task of picking the employees in the bottom 10%. The employees would have known themselves and the managers could have instantly provided the report to their supervisors. Many of our public and private schools provide real time assessments of their students. We're bringing that same methodology into the workplace.

"Now let's talk about discipline. When an employee performs at less than 80%, we start a three-step corrective action plan. First of all, everyone here knows that we want scores that are 75% or better. Less than this and they know they are C level employees and they will be the first to go. When a score hits 75%, we simply ask them what they think the consequence should be if they hit that same number next week, or the next time they agree to meet. Usually the employee will prescribe disciplinary measures that are worse than you may come up with on your own. If they miss it a second time, we ask them what should happen if they miss it three times in a row. Let me give you a real life example. We had a facilities manager here who wasn't hitting his expectations. His manager had sat down with him and they both came up with the minimum expectations to fulfill the duties of the job. It was the simple job description with expectations by date from Step Two. The facilities manager agreed that he could do the minimum requirements. These were pretty simple things, either he did them or he didn't. He agreed that if he couldn't do them after three chances, he would leave his keys on the table and resign. For the first two weeks he provided some excuses for why he couldn't accomplish the tasks at hand. When we asked what should happen if he missed it a third week in a row, he again said he'd leave. He resigned after the third week. We were not the bad guys. He admitted he was incapable of meeting the minimum requirements for the job. With this system, an employer should never have to fire another employee. They will fire themselves," Blake said with a smile.

## POSITIVE CONSEQUENCES

"Todd, it's more important that we provide the right response when the employee hits their goal than the discipline when they don't. You already know that people respond better to positive responses than negative. So when an employee reaches 80% of their expectations, we praise them. Remember, the role of the supervisor is that of a mentor. When you look at the attributes of a mentor, they are synonymous with the roles of a parent. Employees want to please their supervisors in the same way children want to please their parents. They want to meet the parents' expectations and when they do, they want affectionate praise. We're not going to give hugs and kisses to our employees for doing a good job, but we will shake their hand and tell them they are a valuable member of our team. This component is a key ingredient to employees enjoying whom they work with. Much in the way that children will enjoy being with their parents if they please them on a regular basis and vice versa. If the parent only dictates and disciplines, then the child will not want to please the parent and will just want the provision. "Just give me food, clothes, roof and transportation I need to survive and the moment I'm able, I'm out of here," is the attitude of a child whose parents don't understand what they really want. Children want parents who pursue them, seek to please them and meet their needs. I can't emphasize this enough. We want to be an encouraging place to work, so we strive to reward good work. We don't take good work for granted. Make sure you get this," Blake said firmly as he looked deep into Todd's eyes.

## Chapter Summary

- The maximum number of people who report to you should be less than 30.

- One-on-One 50/50 Meetings should take place once a week.

  — Every other week will work; weekly is best.

- The meeting should take place during the slowest part of your day and week.

- You can hold a 50/50 Meeting anywhere, as long as it allows focused attention on each other.

- The ideal meeting is 20–30 minutes. But even a five-minute meeting is okay.

- Your 50/50 Meetings will only be with the people that directly report to you.

- Remember your "role" as a coach before you start your meeting.

- Everyone should be holding 50/50 Meetings.

- The first half of a One-on-One Meeting is to set and align expectations.

- Use the Filter for maximum effectiveness.

- There is a grading system for performance.

- There are consequences for performance—good and bad.

**POINTS TO PONDER**

- How many people report to your boss in addition to you?

- How many people report to you?

- Are you holding One-on-Ones on a regular basis (weekly)?

- Are you clear about what you need to accomplish as well as what you won't be accomplishing?

- How about for those who report to you?

- When people do a good job, do you encourage them with accolades?

- When people don't perform according to expectations, what are the consequences? Who sets them?

# 16

# The One-On-One
# 50/50 Meeting, Part II

"OKAY TODD, now that we've thoroughly discussed the left side of the equation for the One-on-Ones, now we'll talk about the right side. First, it's extremely important that you conduct your One-on-Ones in this order. First you agree on what they need to do to be successful in their position—the left side. Then you make sure they are capable of doing it—the right side. You want the person to leave saying, 'He showed me exactly what I needed to do to be successful in my position and then he genuinely was interested in me as a person.' In the Group meeting, the goal is for people to get to know each other on more than an acquaintance level and to go over the rules. In the One-on-One, the goal is to determine if there's anything happening in the person's life that would prevent them from being successful and that we might help them through," Blake explained.

"So here's how you do it. Once you've aligned expectations, you need to put away your work papers and just talk about life. You can simply start with the question, 'How are things going for you?' We are not going to pry into a person's private life any more than they want to share. However, I can tell you that if you show an interest, nearly everyone wants to share their successes and failures with you. It's human nature. People want to share their pains and their gains with the people around them, especially their friends. So you can start by simply asking, 'What was the best thing that happened this past week?' Followed by, 'What was the worst thing that happened this past week?' People want a venue to share what they're excited about and sometimes what they are unhappy about. We don't pry, we only ask the vague question. They can respond however they want," Blake told him.

## EARN TRUST, DON'T VIOLATE IT

"Todd, you will need to earn the trust of the people who report to you. You will very quickly find that some people can't wait to unload their biggest problems. As the mentor, coach or parent role we take, you need to understand how to deal with some of the information. People will trust you with confidences that are sometimes sensitive in nature. The world doesn't need to know about some of the things you hear. When employees tell you something, you need to ask them what can be shared with their team and which things they prefer didn't leave the room. This is extremely important. This often goes sideways in companies when an employee shares something in confidence with another employee who then tells someone else. Pretty soon a gossip chain starts and there are many unhappy and hurt people. We don't allow that here. You need to be crystal clear with your employees. If someone tells you something, you must get their permission to tell others if it's necessary to include the others in helping the person through a season. That is of course unless it's illegal or must be reported to the proper authorities. If you hear anything related to child abuse or physical abuse of another person or animal, you must inform the person that this has to be reported to the police. Then pick up the phone and call the police. Hopefully this won't happen very often and you will only get the other kinds of problems people have.

"Let me give you a real life example. We had an employee, Janice, who came to me and told me her husband had a drug and gambling problem. She was a good employee but we saw the signs in her performance. She finally told us during a One-on-One what was going on and that she didn't want her fellow employees to know. We agreed that we would tell the employees that Janice was simply going through a difficult season in her life and that she needed our support. We treated it exactly the same as the dying parent and the wedding seasons we've already talked about. We gave Janice time off for counseling appointments and at other times when she had to deal with the situation. After a few months, Janice told us she was getting a divorce. We told her team that her situation was going from bad to worse and that she would need even more support. The team didn't know details and respected her desire to keep the problem to herself. Eventually she was able to tell her co-workers who were filling in for her while she was dealing with attorneys and a broken heart. We supported her through the process and a few years later Janice remarried. Who do you think was in her wedding?" Blake asked.

Todd shook his head.

"They were her two teammates who were doing her job while she was going through the divorce," Blake replied.

"The point is we need to hold certain things in confidence and agree on exactly what we will say to other people if we need their help. Because we've been doing this program here for some time, everyone understands the One-on-One meeting. It was in the very beginning we had to earn trust and get agreement that at times people will need to keep things confidential and other times they will be looking for their co-workers to help them through a season. This had to be done on a one-on-one basis. We learned the hard way that we couldn't announce the company is introducing a new program to help everyone through their personal problems. If we did that, we would have employees giving reasons why they couldn't perform that week. They'd look for the company and their co-workers to help them through everyday struggles. Instead we simply started the program and individually asked people in their One-on-Ones how things were going in their lives."

## THE TEN RELATIONSHIPS

"Todd, when we first started, our people didn't know what to talk about in their One-on-Ones. Both the supervisors and the employees didn't know how to get past, 'Nice weather we're having,' or 'How are the wife and kids?' I had come across some great material on the subject by Dr. Gil Stieglitz (you can find his material at www.ptlb.com). He determined that one could start a conversation with anybody by going through what he called the ten relationships in life. They are:

1. God
2. Self
3. Marriage
4. Family
5. Work
6. Church
7. Money
8. Society
9. Friends
10. Enemies

All you had to do was ask a gentle question about any one of these ten relationships and eventually you learn what that person is most interested in talking about. For example, you could ask, 'What's your hobby?' This is a very simple or gentle question about self. 'How do you enjoy spending your time?' This points directly to which of the ten relationships people most focus on. Dr. Stieglitz has an interesting perspective on these ten relationships. He views them as orchards in our lives, each one requiring a certain amount of cultivation to produce fruit. Unless we give attention to each one, the orchard could wither and die. Often people get out of balance because they put all their energy into one or two orchards and let the rest die. Then they wonder why they died. For example, if we see that someone is a workaholic, we know they are out of balance. They are spending too much time in the work orchard and others are suffering. I encourage you to look at these and do a quick assessment. Are you giving each orchard enough attention for it to bear good fruit? If any orchard isn't doing well, you probably need to spend some time there to regain the balance.

"It's very important that you don't pry into someone's personal life nor state your opinion about what they tell you. If someone wants to talk about a subject that is of a personal nature, such as sex, God, family situations, etc., it is important you understand the laws we are guided by and our company policies. We are an equal opportunity employer and we will not discriminate against anyone for his or her religious preferences, sexual preferences, age, gender, political affiliation or other characteristics we could discriminate against. If employees are in a season of life and we can help them through as a fellow human being, we want to do that. But we need to use good judgment in the process. We won't allow people to take advantage of us and we won't tolerate people making their problems our problems. You will find it's a fine line we walk. In general, there are a few tests you can run to see if getting involved makes sense, or if the person is trying to use us."

## THE EIGHT TESTS TO GOOD DECISION MAKING

"Whenever I face a tough decision, I refer to these tests. I've found it helps when people come to me with their problems that I can walk them through the tests. I also use these tests to determine if we, as a company, need to help the person through the season.

1   As you ponder the problem, do you get a strong sense about the direction you should take?

2   If you were to consult books that gave great advice on the issue, what would the advice be?

3   If you talked to two or three people in positions of authority on the topic, what would they advise?

4   If you talked to two or three people who were very wise, what would they advise?

5   Is there a logical opportunity for resolve?

6   Are the provisions available for the resolve?

7   Does it make sense?

8   If you are married, what does your spouse say?

Todd, these are tests we use to answer difficult decisions. We use the CAP tests on the cursory level and we use these eight tests as a more thorough test in addition to the CAP test. Both have served us well and have kept us from making some major mistakes. So in the case of Francis, if we heard her situation for the first time and ran them through the tests, the method we chose to resolve it made more sense than telling her to get to work on time and keep her head in the game. If we ran our decision to give her Wednesdays off through these tests, it would have been crystal clear we were making the best decision. Let's compare that to someone we believe wants to take advantage of our goodwill. Say a team member came into your office and told you she was going through a tough time. She can't pay her bills, can't keep her car running properly, and isn't eating very well. All of this leads to continual tardiness and absences. Yet you've observed her spending money foolishly on clothes and drinks after work. What do you think the eight tests would tell us?"

"The first test alone would give the answer," Todd reasoned.

"Exactly. She's not in a bad season, she's giving excuses!

"Though it may seem old fashioned, I encourage everyone to use the Golden Rule. Treat others how you would like to be treated. Do what's best for the other person. In the example I just gave, perhaps discipline is the best solution. You encourage them to meet the minimum standards by being more responsible with their income, not going to the bar on the way home, or spending too much money on themselves."

Todd felt a little convicted. He regularly stopped by his club on the way home to have drinks with his buddies. He instantly rationalized it as spending time on the 'friends' orchard. But deep down he knew it came at the expense of his wife and kids. He knew from his very brief encounter with Severson's ethics program that if he furthered one thing at the expense of another, it was unethical. He remembered that by going home on Fridays right after work and spending some time with his family he was seeing good results in his 'family' orchard. Perhaps he should rethink the bar thing.

## LIVING IN THE 85%

Blake continued, "There's one thing relating to Step Three I want to leave you with. I call it the 85%. My experience has been that people have a choice about which emotional sphere they live in. They can live in the positive sphere or the negative sphere. You can instantly tell which one a person lives in when you ask them how things are going or by what they generally talk about throughout the day. Do they talk about the bad stuff in life or the good stuff? Are they living in the 85% or the 15%? Let me explain further. If you were to do an overall assessment of your life by making a list of everything you have going for you and everything against you, what would that list look like? What percent would be positive and what percent would be negative?" Blake asked.

"I've done this test with hundreds of people and generally speaking, most people would say their life is 85% positive and 15% negative. When they take into account the country we live in, the quality of our food, water, air, the freedoms we have, the healthcare system, protection from our enemies and the general provisions for life that are available to us, the bottom line is we are in a pretty good place. Compare it to other parts of the world and we have it really good. I agree that for every one of us, there are things in our lives that are really bad. People get sick and die. People divorce each other or go bankrupt. Bad people take advantage of other people. There's a lot of crud out there. Still, when people do an assessment and look at where they are compared to the how it could be, most people would agree that life's pretty good—about 85% of it. However, we live in a nation where we only hear about the 15%. Newspapers, television and radio stations generally focus on the 15% that's gone very wrong. We are indoctrinated by the bad news to the extent that we start living in the 15%. All we can talk about is what's not working right, who's been taken advantage of or who is in a bad place. We complain about the 15% more than we recognize the 85%. It can become our personality. So where do you want to live?" Blake asked.

Before Todd could answer, Blake continued, "We want employees here to live in the 85%. If we choose to focus on better things, we will have a better environment. But it takes discipline. We face two problems. First, when we do our 50/50 Meetings, we are generally looking at what's preventing us from accomplishing our goals. We focus on the 15%. Second, if someone is in a season, it's difficult for him or her to think about anything but the 15%. So we need to keep things in perspective. That's one reason we do our 50/50 Meetings in a specific order—success in work first, where we might address how to work through the 15% items and then our personal life. Our experience has been that we encounter seasons less than 10% of the time. This means that for 90% of your One-on-Ones, you will talk about the positive things that people are doing in their lives—hobbies, families, community involvement, and the things in their life that are going well. It's important that we leave our One-on-Ones encouraging people to get back into the 85%. Even the people in seasons can be gently moved in that direction by pointing out the other positive areas of life. When people are in the darkest of despair, there is still something positive they can appreciate. You just have to find it. There may be times when it feels like everyone is in a season on your team. You need to move forward, looking for positive things in the day. You may go through a season yourself and need the support of your boss. It's often difficult to help the people on your team when you're knee deep in a problem. If that happens, you need to let us help you through the season."

## A Two Way Street

"Todd, one last thing you need to know. For you to be an authentic person, you will have to pull from some of your life experiences to share with people. I'm not asking anyone to talk about private parts of life, but at times we can easily associate our employee's season with something we have gone through. If you have experience in your life that can bring perspective to your employee's situation, bring it up. If you think you're above the problems of your employees and they sense it in your demeanor, the relationship won't be as good as it could be. You need to be authentic with the people around you. We all have problems and we can help each other through them. I've done this with you as I explained how I went through the drills with my wife and kids. If we aren't real, we live under the façade that so many people unfortunately do.

"Well Todd, we've covered a lot today discussing Step Three. It's the most important part of our program. It's what sets us apart as a company because Relational Intelligence is the tool we use to meet our employees' number one goal—to enjoy the people they work with. When we become relationally intelligent, people are happier, more productive and more reliable. As usual, I want you to take what you've learned home and share it with your family. Every aspect of Step Three can be applied to them. See if you can figure out what I mean by that and we'll discuss it next Friday."

Todd went home that evening and met with Sarah and the kids. He explained Step Three of the program and had already decided to try having One-on-One 50/50s with them on a regular basis. They understood Step Three, thought it made sense and remained interested as they discussed it through dinner.

## CHAPTER SUMMARY

- The order of the One-on-One is vital: left side first, then right side.

- The goal of the second half of the meeting is to determine if there's something that would prevent accomplishment of the goals.

- If there is something, then we need to support people through the issues.

- We want to treat and support others how we want to be treated and supported.

- People will open up only if they know it's a safe environment and their confidence in you won't be violated.

- There are ten orchards in our life: God, Self, Marriage, Family, Work, Church, Society, Money, Friends and Enemies.
  - We must keep each of these "orchards" in balance so they don't die.
  - We can begin a conversation by asking "gentle questions" about each of the ten relationships until we find the one they are most interested in.

- There are eight tests we can use for making good decisions (p. 200)
  - For major decisions in your life, don't think it will work with four or five out of the eight.

- We have a choice on our frame of mind.
  - Is the cup half empty or half full?

- An important part of Relational Intelligence is sharing experiences in life and learning from each other.

## POINTS TO PONDER

- When you have learned people were going through seasons, have you helped and encouraged them through that season?
  - How?
- Are you good at holding confidential information to yourself?
  - If not, how will you ever earn trust from people?
- How are you doing on the ten orchards in your life?
  - Are they all healthy?
  - Are any out of balance, withering and dying?
- What might you do to re-cultivate an orchard that might need attention?
- Will you use the eight tests for good decision-making?
  - Don't settle for four or five out of the eight.
- Do you tend to look at the glass as half empty or half full?
  - Are you a pessimist or an optimist?
  - Do you agree with the 85% rule?
- Are you willing to share your experiences with others, especially if it could prevent them from making the same mistake or gaining the same positive result?
- Are you willing to have One-on-One 50/50s with your family and friends?

# 17

# Customers, Vendors, and Others

THE FOLLOWING WEEK, Todd and Blake met at their normal time. Blake started by asking Todd how things had gone with his family discussion. Todd reported that they understood it and were interested. Blake explained some important points to Todd. The first was that with family and friends it shouldn't be programmatic. He shouldn't go home and say, "To have a happy and successful family and marriage, we're going to have weekly One-on-One 50/50s. We will meet each Saturday morning and go through the lists of things that need to be done around the house, prioritize them, weight them and then score them. Then we will spend an equal amount of time making sure you are okay as a person and determine if anything would prevent you from accomplishing your responsibilities as wife, husband, father, etc."

"That would be senseless," Blake pointed out. "We need to be genuine and sincere in our desires to understand what we all face in life as we go through our days."

Next, Blake began to teach Todd how the program applied to their customers, vendors and literally everyone they came in contact with.

"Todd, today I want to talk about the *Right Side of the Equa-*

*tion* as it relates to our customers and vendors. You see, our customers have exactly the same long-term desires as our employees. They want to enjoy the people they work with, both in terms of their own employees as well as their vendors and their customers. It all goes back to what's important in life. Remember the top three priorities? One is having people in our life that we enjoy. Intellectual stimulation is often a priority as well and we accomplish that most often through our work. So if we know our customers want to enjoy the people they work with, and by extension buy from, then we can apply the program to them as well. All three steps can be applied.

"First, we need to understand their goals and objectives. What is it they need from us and what are their expectations? This is fairly simple in our business. We sell products that people need for their cars. They can buy our products or someone else's. For most people it comes down to a price/quality/availability decision. Understanding that, we need to provide them with a product that is of good quality, guaranteed to be available when they need it and at a cost that provides them with an adequate profit. Simple, right? Well what happens when our competitor shows up with the exact same solution? Their products provide the same price/quality/availability and margin. Then what happens? The buyer either tries to get a better price or will make a decision based on something else. I can tell you right now it will be the person he likes the most. The one he enjoys doing business with. And my experience is the people factor has more bearing on it than you might expect. I know people will sometimes give up price, quality, availability or margin because they like the person and enjoy spending time with them. But it's often the exception and you shouldn't count on it. Therefore, Step One is still important. You need to determine the top four or five things your customer wants to accomplish, in priority order and the weight of each item. We want to have a written set of goals from each of our customers. We want to ask the same question you asked Sarah about being her dream husband. We want you to ask your customers to name the top four or five things that would make us their dream supplier. Then we want the customer to prioritize them and weight them. Then our goal is to meet our customer's needs similar to how you meet the needs of your wife. We've found that when we do that one thing, we are already one step ahead of our competition. Our competitors have never asked what the most important things are to the customer. Can you see how this works?" Blake asked.

"Definitely," Todd replied.

"Second, we need to make sure we have the right person in the right position for the client. The Five Cs are very important to the client. Does our representative have the right Character, Competency, Chemistry, Capability and Contribution for the customer? We want to assess this rather than assume that the body we park in the position is going to be a good fit with each customer in that region. The component that is the most diffi-cult to gauge is Chemistry. We have a pretty good idea when we put someone in the field they have the other four Cs. The one that is purely a personal fit is the Chemistry. So we ask every sales-man to assess their Chemistry with the client and then ask their supervisor to make a call from time to time on the client to make sure the customer is positive on all Five Cs, especially Chemistry. If we sense there's a problem, we bring in one or two of our other people to see if there might be a better fit. Customers will appre-ciate it when you move someone out who has bad Chemistry.

"The other important component to Step Two is to com-municate clear expectations with the customer. What do they need from us by what date for them to feel that we've succeeded? To a certain degree, we do the same thing with them, in a gentle way. We need them to know that for us to be successful in what we do, they need to maintain good communication with us, we need to follow agreed upon policies and procedures and we need to make sure we get paid under the terms we agree to. Each time we meet with our customer, we make sure we agree to a new list of prioritized expectations. Often we will follow up a meeting with an email that memorializes what we discussed.

"As you may have guessed, Step Three is the most important step with our customers as well. We need to hold 50/50 Meetings with them to be successful. Sometimes these meetings will be Group 50/50s, but usually they will be One-on-Ones. The group meetings will take the form of one of our salespeople meeting with a large group or a meeting with many people from both companies to discuss how the two firms will interact. We will follow the same format of making sure we discuss our goals and expectations first, and that will comprise half of the meeting. Then we will take it upon ourselves to see how everyone is doing as a team. We usually ask them how their company is doing, inquire about any new initiatives, or perhaps discuss something we've heard about an employee and how we can encourage that employee back at Severson. We essentially give them a testimony of how we work through similar situations in our company. There is always something we compliment them on, so that we leave with a focus on the 85%," Blake explained.

"Most of our meetings with our customers will be One-on-Ones. Again, we follow the same format. Goals and objectives first followed by how we're doing as people. We do this from the very first time we meet them until the time they move on. My experience is that many salespeople understand the concept of a personal relationship, but make a mistake right off the bat and reverse the order. The order is key. You have to discuss the goals and objectives first."

"Why is this so important?" asked Todd.

"Here's why. Everyone feels like they are the busiest person on earth. The last thing they have time for is a salesperson. If for some reason they do give an appointment to a salesperson, that employee has about two minutes to say something that makes them want to keep listening. The customer will have no desire for a relationship with a person he never intends to buy from. So when a salesperson steps in and attempts to either break the ice or establish a personal relationship first, the customer usually stops listening and moves to end the meeting as quickly as possible. But we stick to our 50/50 plan. We understand the two-minute drill and want to make our point for doing business with us first. Here's what we typically start with, 'Thanks for taking the meeting. Let me get right to the point. We manufacture accessories for cars. Our prices are competitive, our quality is very good and we deliver when we say we will deliver. What I believe sets us apart is that you will enjoy doing business with us. We have a specific set of rules we follow.' At this time we either tell them our rules or hand them a business card that has rules on the back. 'We are an Ethical Practices Company, which means we strive for the best practices in all aspects of our business. We would like the opportunity to have you try our products and experience the service and support that comes with dealing with our company.' This usually leads to a variety of questions from the customer and allows us to show them how we seek to determine their top four or five needs and how we will meet those expectations. Usually when the customer sees that we are different because we have a very specific system for determining their needs, we usually get a chance to bid.

"Once the business objectives are completed and it would appear that the meeting is done, then I move to the second half of the 50/50 Meeting. Even if it's on the way out and is not truly 50/50, I will seek to know more about the person. I then note the things in his or her office and ask about them. Most people will have a photograph of their family, hobby or special interest. You just have to ask about it after you know they want to do business with you and then they will usually start talking. If they don't have anything obvious to ask about, I usually ask them, 'So what do you do for fun?' It's a simple and innocuous question that can show you where their interests lie. I usually then tell them something about me that allows them to know I'm a person, not a machine. If they talk about their family indicating that is important to them, then I will tell them about my family. If they want to talk about their hobbies, then I will tell them about my hobbies or I will at least learn more about their hobbies. I actually find it fascinating to hear what people are passionate about. Then once I know what they're interested in, I know what to start the conversation with in my next 50/50 Meeting. If someone talks to me about their family, then next time I will naturally ask how their family is doing after we've done the first part of the meeting.

"We know that our customers will go through the same good and bad seasons as our employees. So why wouldn't we want to do the same thing for them that we're willing to do for our employees? Customers will get sick, some will die, some will have babies and some will get married. When you show concern and a desire to help them through that, they will appreciate it. But be careful—you'll be setting a trend that nobody else is doing. Our society teaches the opposite. We are taught to pay attention only to ourselves and not to look out for our friends, neighbors, acquaintances or business associates. Severson Systems wants to treat them how we would want to be treated. We want to celebrate their good seasons with them and we want to come to their assistance in bad times. We've found the smallest things help tremendously. We've visited our customers in the hospital when they've had babies, car accidents or serious illnesses. It's surprising to them that you would care enough to visit them. In fact, the first time I visit a customer in the hospital, they're shocked. They can't believe I actually came to show them care and concern. And the moment they determine that you sincerely care, it's a whole new ballgame. They will go out of their way to help you succeed at what you're doing. Admittedly, at first we may have gone to help build the relationship, but as time went by we actually enjoyed the process of helping or celebrating with them far more than the future financial successes that came from it. That's why I told you when we first met that we are about more than money and climbing ladders. You see, what happens in the process is that you will be meeting your number one need as well. Your number one desire is to enjoy the people you work with, including customers, and when that need is met in a natural and deep way, that payoff becomes far more important than the money. Don't make the mistake of saying you don't want to bother them in their time of trouble or joy. People appreciate those who show them genuine interest, care and concern. Yet many mistakenly take the attitude that they should not visit the hospital because they do not have an invitation. It doesn't occur to the patient to extend an invitation to their representative from Severson, who they barely know, to come visit them. They don't want to impose on your life and it wouldn't even hit their radar screen as they are in the midst of whatever turmoil or joy they are in the hospital for. Your visit can be short and sweet. 'I

THE RIGHT SIDE OF THE EQUATION

just wanted to stop by and bring you flowers and cookies and see if there was anything I could do for you?' As with the employee, just asking the question is huge."

## It's the Same with Vendors

"Okay, I've gone over the program with customers, now let's talk for just a moment about our vendors—the people we buy goods and services from. We do the exact same thing with them. In any meeting we can dictate how it goes. When someone attempts to sell something to us for the first time, we will ask that they get right to the point and explain why we should do business with them. I usually ask them to give me their 30-second elevator speech on what they do and why anyone should use their goods or services. I'm always surprised at how many people don't have this speech down. If it's not compelling and I think we have what they are offering covered very well somewhere else, I'll save them time and my time, too. I'll politely excuse them and thank them for stopping by. If they say something compelling that peaks my interest, then I will give them what my top four or five priorities are for potentially buying their product or service and what I expect of them to get my business. Then once we've gone through the goals and expectations, I will start a 50/50 Meeting with them. I want to know something about them, how and why they work for the company, what their hobbies are and how they spend their spare time. In that process I'm forming an opinion about whether I like them, if they have the Five Cs and if I would like to work with them, regardless of what their proposal looks like. When they come back, I'll have made a note about the things we talked about and we will start forming a relationship. If something happens in their life, we show them the same support that we do with our employees and customers. In doing this, we've

214

built very strong relationships with our vendors, many of which have stepped up to the plate in a big way to help us when we've needed it. They've helped us get a special price when we needed to be more competitive. They've gone out of their way to meet a delivery deadline when it didn't seem possible, and they've even introduced us to some new clients. More business between our companies is very desirable because we enjoy working with each other," Blake explained.

It all made such good sense to Todd, yet he had never really thought about it in this way.

## FRIENDS AND FAMILY PLAN

"Todd, this program works in all aspects of life. We started talking about how it works for our employees, but then I showed you how it works for our customers and vendors. I had you explain it to your family and you've incorporated perhaps a little there. The bottom line is that the program provides the essential components necessary to be in a relationship with anyone. To be in a relationship, you only need to know that both parties have needs. If you simply ask them what their needs are and then do your best to meet some of those needs, you will build a relationship. It's been my experience that when you seek to meet the needs of others, you will naturally meet some of your own needs. If they are aware of them, they will naturally seek to meet some of your needs too.

"Todd, use the plan at home. Get the goals from your kids of what a great Hanson family household looks like and what they would like to accomplish for the next year. Then get their lists of the five to ten things that would make you their dream dad. Meet with them on a regular basis and give them the attention that they want and need. We've had many people who thought their relationships were too far gone with their wife and kids even to begin to do these drills. Yet when an effort is made to improve things and both parties recognize that it would be better to work through the tough stuff rather than throw in the towel, the pay-off is great.

"Do the same thing with Sarah. I'm not sure if you've had a great marriage for all the years you've been married, but if your goal is for it to grow and thrive, this program works. When you show her that you take her list seriously and incorporate it into your daily activity, she will appreciate it. Do the 50/50 Meetings with Sarah and your kids. Unless you actually meet and spend time with them, you can't possibly be meeting their needs. Spending time with them is perhaps the biggest component in Relational Intelligence."

On the outside Todd was fine. He nodded and gave the façade that everything he was hearing was really great. On the inside, he was hurting. He had been thinking about his marriage and all the lost time with his kids and wife. All that energy spent on stuff that doesn't even matter now. Yet his kids are almost grown and out of the house and his marriage has some deep scars. Had he thought about meeting with his wife and kids each year and making goals for the family, had he gotten a list of the top ten needs for his wife and kids each year and had he spent some one-on-one time each week with each of them—things would be very different now. Much different.

Blake sensed the façade and asked Todd what he was think-ing. He knew that it was likely Todd had some of the problems that occur in families when you don't have a program like this, so he said to him, "You know, Todd, the good thing about this program is that it's never too late to start it. You may have some remorse for not taking care of some of the orchards earlier in your life, but you now you have a choice. You can either embrace the program and begin to incorporate it into your life, or you can go on with the way things were."

Though he didn't feel a whole lot better, it did make sense. He knew he had to implement the program in his personal life as well as his professional life. He knew deep down inside that life would improve. Life already had improved in a measurable way at home. As Blake walked Todd to his door that week, he encouraged him to be dedicated to the program and not to expect big changes instantly. It is a process.

## Chapter Summary

- One-on-Ones shouldn't be programmatic with your family and friends.

- The *Right Side of the Equation* applies to our customers, vendors, and literally everyone we come in contact with—especially our friends and family.

- People will make decisions based on whom they like best if all other things are equal.

- If you ask the people around you what's important to them, in what order, and with what weight, they will normally tell you. Then you simply have to live up to their expectation.

- The Five Cs are important to everyone.

- Customers and vendors have expectations relating to "what does it turn into by when."
  - It's very important to determine what that is for your customers and vendors.

- The order for the customer 50/50 Meeting is just as important as with the employee 50/50.
  - Define success relating to work first.
  - Discuss the personal side of life second.

- When meeting someone in business for the first time, don't waste his or her time. Get right to the point.
  - Determine the top four or five most important things to your customer or vendor.
  - Put them in priority order and give them a weight. Nobody else does this.

- Customers and vendors will go through the same seasons, good and bad, as you and your employees will. You can help them through their seasons, too.

- Don't be afraid to lead people into a 50/50 Meeting when they want to do business or get to know you.

- Ask vendors to tell you in 30 seconds or less why you need to do business with them.

- Prioritize what will make them successful in working with you, and weight each item.

## POINTS TO PONDER

- Will you consider the 50/50 Meeting with everyone you come in contact with?

- Do you waste people's time by trying to establish a relationship first?
  - Can you reverse the order and see if there's a reason to be there first?

- As your customers and vendors go through seasons, will you help them just as you would someone in your family?

# Companywide Deployment of the Program

## 18

**T**HE FOLLOWING WEEK BLAKE TOLD TODD he was down to the final details of learning the program. But learning it and deploying it were two different things just as teaching the fundamentals of golf and playing golf are different. The first few swings can be pretty funny.

There were two weeks left in Blake's schedule to spend with Todd. This week he would cover how the program is taught and deployed throughout the company plus a few other management techniques used at Severson. The next week Blake would go over the scorecard system they use to measure how people are doing.

"Todd, today I want to explain to you how we've deployed the program throughout our company. We've taught the program to a few other companies and know this deployment system works. First, the top person in the division, team or company must accept the program. This person needs to understand and accept the premises of the program and have a desire to deploy it himself. Then that person learns it and teaches it to his direct reports. His direct reports learn and practice the program with their supervisor and then teach it to the people that report to them, and so on. Essentially, one level teaches it to the next level

and then the next level until the entire company has implemented the program. We've learned that there is a logical order to the
deployment. We've even created an annual calendar for timely
execution. The program is taught over the first six to eight weeks,
and then deployed throughout the remainder of the year. Here's
a copy of the annual calendar so you can see how this works
throughout the year."

| SEVERSON SYSTEMS | THE RIGHT SIDE OF THE EQUATION ANNUAL PROGRAM CALENDAR |
|---|---|
| Week 1 | Overview of the program |
| Week 2 | Define and Refine your corporate and personal Goals and Objectives |
| Week 3 | Define and Refine your Job/Plan Descriptions |
| Week 4 | Define your Weekly, Quarterly and Annual Accomplishments/Expectations |
| Week 5 | Hold a Team Meeting – Establish Rules and hold Group 50/50 Meeting |
| Week 6 | Start One-on-One 50/50 Meetings with your team |
| Week 7 | Juniors, Accountability Partners and Best Friends |
| Week 8 | Complete the Baseline Scorecards |
| Week 10 | Evaluate scorecards and align expectations |
| Week 12 | Quarterly Planning – What needs work |
| Week 14 | New Quarterly Goals – Team Alignment |
| Week 16 | Reality Check – What's working/What's not |
| Week 18 | Calibrate with Spouse/Children/Team Leaders |
| Week 20 | Review Rules/Relationships/Responsibilities |
| Week 22 | Quarterly Reviews/Scorecards Due |
| Week 24 | Quarterly Planning – What needs work |
| Week 26 | New Quarterly Goals – Team Alignment |
| Week 28 | Reality Check – What's working/What's not |
| Week 30 | Calibrate with Spouse/Children/Team Leaders |
| Week 32 | Review Rules/Relationships/Responsibilities |
| Week 34 | Quarterly Reviews/Scorecards Due |
| Week 36 | Quarterly Planning – What needs work |
| Week 38 | New Quarterly Goals – Team Alignment |
| Week 40 | Reality Check – What's working/What's not |
| Week 42 | Calibrate with Spouse/Children/Team Leaders |
| Week 44 | Review Rules/Relationships/Responsibilities |
| Week 46 | Quarterly Reviews/Scorecards Due |
| Week 48 | Quarterly Planning – What needs work |
| Week 50 | New Quarterly Goals – Team Alignment |
| Week 52 | Reality Check – What's working/What's not |

"As you can see, we look at our year in terms of quarters. This calendar is a roadmap for individual and group meetings. The calendar also incorporates a check and balance system into the program. So far you know the program requires weekly meetings where you calibrate expectations with your employees. Our annual calendar adds another layer of responsibility. It's a system to check and re-evaluate how things are going. As you can see, we want you to begin scorecards in week ten and complete them quarterly to assess how things are going. Based on those scores, we want you to reassess where you are in relation to your annual goals. At week 12, we're asking you to revise your quarterly plans based on what's working well and what's not. Halfway into every new quarter, we want you to do an assessment of how things are going with your team—you'll see that in week 16. Then on a quarterly basis we want to remind everyone here to keep putting an effort toward the home front. We do that by encouraging employees to reassess their goals with their families as well as with the people in the office. Finally, in addition to incorporating discussions about our rules on a weekly basis, we're asking everyone to review the rules and ethics program materials they covered during the past quarter. We've found that when we discuss our rules and ethics weekly and hold a quarterly meeting to talk about everything we've learned, it has a better chance of sticking in the minds of our employees. Most companies have strategic plans or business plans. Few have annual calendars that hold them accountable to achieving their goals or plans. I firmly believe that if you want to be successful, you need a discipline to hold you to it. Otherwise it tends to be forgotten.

"The calendar also helps with our strategic planning. At the beginning of the year we set annual goals and objectives. Each person then sets their goals for the year in alignment with our corporate goals. Each member of the team should be able to explain his or her contribution to the big picture and why the company may not be able to reach the annual goal without them.

"It may take a week or two for a division or company to go through the process of determining what their goals are for the year. For example, each year we hire outside consultants to help us develop strategic plans and annual goals. That process takes a few weeks by the time we get input from key people on the management team and then integrate that with the consultant's process. Once we complete that process, then we can plug those strategic objectives and annual goals right into this program in Step One. Next, it takes a few weeks for a manager to work through the process of who he will need to fulfill the strategic plan. Remember, he needs to be able to support and defend why each person is on the team and how he wouldn't be able to meet the annual plan if they weren't on the team. That may be a culture change for many companies who plug bodies into positions instead of knowing the strengths and weaknesses of each person on the team. It can really take the steam out of a team when people are plugged in who are incompetent or are put into a position simply because they have been there for years. Instead, employees should be reassigned into positions where they can add value by accomplishing something of value for the organization. When you put the wrong person into a position, it becomes difficult for others to succeed because those who aren't accomplishing anything for the team can bring the whole team down. This also happens when a company puts a favored relative into a position that really can't do the job. It also is common in municipalities or government posts where people are tenured into positions but have stopped working for all practical purposes. That's the person who simply has run out of gas but needs pay and somehow feels entitled to keep working because of the many prior years of faithful service. They forgot that they were already paid for those years and they are not entitled to an extended payout. We talked about this when I covered Contribution.

"Todd, there's one other interesting thing we've learned about the program relating to its deployment—it can be forced one level up. What I mean is, we've had supervisors from other companies work in our factory as outside contractors for extended periods of time. In that process, they've been taught the program from some of our staff members. Then they've gone back to their own companies and asked for a top down implementation. For whatever reason, the owners didn't want to deploy the program so the supervisor did it anyway within his department or division. In that process, he had no problem making his boss participate in the program because he simply started by defining their goals, and then went through the same process we've developed for choosing the right team and clarifying specific responsibilities. Then he started weekly or bi-weekly One-on-Ones with his team and his boss and found a way to incorporate the rules. That division of the company consistently had the highest performance and income, and the owner really liked the way the supervisor was running his department. Eventually the supervisor was able to deploy the program on a companywide basis. It works even if people won't formally adopt the program. I'm telling you this because you may explain the program to a vendor or even your wife and they may choose to implement it where they work."

## JUNIORS, PARTNERS, AND BEST FRIENDS

"Okay Todd, there are three more management initiatives we use here at Severson that you need to know about. One is the Junior Program, another is the Accountability Partner Program and the third is the Best Friend Program.

"Let's start with the Junior Program. I'm not sure if you're a sports fan, but you've certainly heard about the concept of first string, second string and so on. This is essentially the Junior Program. Who is on the bench that could instantly move into your spot in the event you are injured, on vacation or taken out completely? It's your junior-- the person on the bench for you. Here at Severson we want every person to have a junior in training that is capable of running onto the field for them so the company doesn't miss a beat. We may not perform as well with the junior, but we won't lose the game," Blake explained.

"In professional sports this concept is done very well. Take basketball, for instance. There are five starters on a basketball team. Those five starters almost never play the entire game. They are taken out for rest periods or because they have too many fouls. When they come out, nobody thinks twice when their junior runs onto the court and picks up where they left off. That's how we want it here. We want everyone inside and outside the company to be aware of our Junior Program and who the junior is for each person. When they see the junior filling in for their senior, it shouldn't even be a concern. The senior must either be on vacation, taking a day off, out sick or doing something else.

"When we first started this program, we didn't have enough depth to have a junior for every person. So there were juniors for multiple people. I was actually the junior for our sales manager, production manager and purchasing manager. Then as we grew, we found we could bring people up from the ranks and begin to teach them the fundamentals of their boss' job.

"There were several unexpected bonuses that came out of this program. It became a very low cost promotion system. For someone to be named the junior to their boss was in fact a promotion of sorts, but it didn't have to come with an increase in pay. We found that we were feeding an employee's desire for intellectual stimulation when we named them a junior and began a training process. Another bonus we hadn't anticipated was the performance and increased productivity component. When employees were asked to train someone as their junior, they improved at their own job. The 'two heads are better than one' motto really began to mean something as the team of the senior and junior started performing at a much higher rate. The junior challenged why certain things were done and our processes improved. The senior person got better because he or she was constantly being watched and had to be deliberate about what they were teaching and doing. It's a terrific system," boasted Blake.

"So let me explain how you begin and maintain this system. First, you agree as a company that you will adopt a Junior Program. You need to announce to the employees that the company is putting the Junior Program in place, so that every employee knows they will be training a junior, no matter how new or low on the totem pole they are. Next you explain that this system is important because we never know when someone might be out sick, have an accident or even die. It makes sense so we can cover for people who need time off for vacations or to attend to personal business. Every employee we've explained the program to thinks it makes good sense and nearly everyone is happy to participate. Once in a while we've found someone who doesn't want to name or train their junior because the company might find out about poor job execution. It would make it easy for the company to replace them with their junior. We view that as another benefit to the program. While those reasons surely do come up, it still makes good sense to have a back up.

"Okay, once you've announced the program and everyone

understands the reason for it, the next step is for each person to name their junior and be able to support and defend why they chose that person. People need to choose a junior who can actually do their job and make a contribution in the position, not just fill the space with a body. Sometimes people will try to pick someone significantly under qualified for the position so they look better. That doesn't fly. Make sure your employees know the person they pick will be a reflection on them and their department. If they pick people who are not competent, it will certainly reflect on the senior.

"Next the employee needs to set up a training schedule and curriculum. The schedule should be set so it doesn't conflict with peak performance times. The curriculum should be simple enough to be understood and complete enough to get the job done. Every employee's senior should review the schedule and curriculum to make sure it makes sense and that the job is being done. The training curriculum is a fairly easy process as the senior can use his or her goals, job description and expectations as the framework and then fill in the details of how he or she accomplishes it. Another added bonus to the Junior Program is that you typically get your processes down on paper," Blake explained.

Todd asked Blake if he had a junior.

"Of course I do," Blake responded. "He's our Vice President of Operations, Kevin Simpson. I feel very confident that if something happened to me, he could easily run the ship until the company could be transitioned. Incidentally, we also have a formal transition plan in place that was designed and implemented by LeadershipOne out of the Sacramento, California area," Blake said with a smile.

"Finally, we have the juniors shadow their seniors on a regular basis and even fill in for them from time to time even when the

senior isn't away from the job. This builds the confidence necessary and helps the rest of the staff, our vendors and our customers become comfortable with the junior. We want to make it so
seamless that on any given day if we see a junior in place we don't
think anything of it. We review the junior's abilities and performance on a quarterly and annual basis through our scorecard
system you will hear about next week."

## ACCOUNTABILITY PARTNERS

"The next thing I want to tell you about is our Accountability
Partner Program. Because we are dedicated to our rules and eth-
ics program we decided we needed an accountability system.
We set up employees in teams of two as accountability partners.
We allow the employees to choose their accountability partner.
There are a variety of reasons we need this program. First, I figured out the hard way that we all have blind spots. Remember
I told you about first starting this program and asking some of
my employees for feedback? I had several blind spots. I didn't
see the impact some of my actions or statements had on others
around me. As you might know, there's almost no accountability for CEOS in the business world. So I set up the accountability
partner system so we could effectively have a second set of eyes
and ears looking out for us. We often say things that we mean
one way, but people interpret differently. The Accountability
Partner Program is designed to have someone close to you that
can tell you things without the fear that it might be taken the
wrong way. Accountability partners have permission under the
guidelines of the company to communicate with you what they
hear or see you doing. If they suspect something you say or do
might be misinterpreted, they can bring it up to you so you can
fix it before it does any damage. The accountability partner also

has the ability to watch what you're doing and be looking out for you relating to the rules and ethics program. If we all agree that we want to live up to the rules and ethics program we've implemented, then sometimes we will need someone to hold us accountable to those rules and ethics. Sometimes we don't realize we are breaking one or more of the rules and we need that accountability partner to bring it to our attention. In the beginning it's tough to allow accountability into your life, but I can tell you that sometimes we just need a little help along the way. The Accountability Partner Program provides that help.

"Now let me go over a few of the details of how we started it and keep it going. As with the Junior Program, we started with an announcement. We explained that we wanted employees to find another person to hold them accountable. Then we asked that they meet bi-weekly to check in. Each one agrees to be a second set of eyes and ears for the other and watches out for them as well as listens to and watches their behavior. If they see something inconsistent with our rules, ethics program or job performance issues, they can bring it up. Obviously it helps to pick an accountability partner who is in your same department or has a similar job. It doesn't work to pick someone who is a subordinate, as they may not feel they have the authority to say anything. We do invite every member of our company to speak to anyone at any level when it comes to accountability and our rules or ethics." Blake explained.

"There have been some real benefits from the accountability program. First, when an employee's performance changes and we suspect a problem or potential season, one of the first people we go to is their accountability partner. Second, the accountability partner system has allowed employees to form a deeper relationship with someone at work. It is one more building block to establish and create an environment where people can enjoy the people they work with. Finally, when someone is in a season, the accountability partner usually becomes the primary liaison between the person in the season and the company. Our Accountability Partner Program is another necessary component to Relational Intelligence. For most people, their accountability partner becomes a trusted friend. He or she becomes part of a support mechanism. It's a very valuable system," Blake said with confidence.

"I've written one of our Value Discussions on the topic of accountability. I thought you'd like to see it, so I printed a copy."

**WHO ARE YOU ACCOUNTABLE TO?**

Have you ever said, "I wish someone had told me before I made that bad decision?" Or, have you ever known you were walking down a path that was wrong, but just didn't have anyone to talk to? It happens to all of us. There is a solution—an Accountability Partner. Why do you need one? Glad you asked.

Nine times out of ten, you will take the right course of action if you know you have someone to answer to about your decision. You may have heard about the "Announcement Test." To refresh your memory: If you announced your intentions to 100 people of high moral character would they support your decision? Chances are, occasionally they would not support your decision.

For example, your employer makes a mistake on your paycheck in your favor. Do you keep the money? Without the Announcement Test, you might rationalize the mistake and say, "the company can afford it" or "they must have wanted me to have this money." Bottom line is that it's a simple mistake and comes out of your employer's pocket. If you announced your intentions to the 100 people of high moral character, all of them would tell you to report the mistake to the company and let them decide what should be done.

Here's why this is so important. We all have fairly similar values. We all demand honesty of each other. We would like loyalty from everyone we know (friends, customers, spouses, vendors, etc.). Nobody wants to be cheated or stolen from. Everyone wants respect. We all want these things, yet sometimes we don't always give them in return. Sometimes we stumble and violate one of those same values that we expect from everyone else.

That's where the Announcement Test and the Accountability Partner come in. If you knew that you had to run every decision past 100 people of the highest character, you may make some different decisions. You wouldn't have been rude to the person who cut you off or pushed in front of you. You wouldn't keep the extra change you get by mistake, and you would never lie.

While it's impossible to think you could actually announce every thought or every action to 100 people, it is possible to consider just one person - your Accountability Partner. This is someone who is not your spouse or significant other, but rather someone of the same sex who can and will hold you truly accountable for all your actions. Make it a two way street. Hold your partner accountable for his or her own actions as well.

Try it. Pick someone you can trust—someone to whom you would entrust your life savings or a life or death decision. Ask that person to become your Accountability Partner. Explain that you would like to meet regularly to tell each other what's going on in your lives. Explain that the goal is to help each other make the right decisions and choices. Good, honest, and moral decisions. The same ones that conform to how you want to be treated by others.

For most people, this is a very difficult step. It's hard to have someone hold you accountable, especially when doing the right thing is harder than the wrong thing. However, difficult steps lead to the greatest accomplishment and change in your life. Give it a try.

## YOUR BEST FRIEND

"The last thing I want to talk to you about today, Todd, is our Best Friend Program. As we've grown, we've always said we want to grow with employees just like the ones already employed here. We like our employees and they are doing a great job for us. We want our employees to feel this is the best possible place to work—the kind of place they wished all their friends could work. So we simply formalized that idea. We put a lot of time and energy into choosing our employees and we've found most of their friends are very similar to them. So we started a system in which we've asked every employee here to make a list of two or three friends they can't wait to have come on board. We then ask them to invite those friends to the plant from time to time so they know who we are and vice versa. Sometimes they'll just stop by during a coffee break and other times our employees will bring them over on their day off. As we've needed people, we go right to our employees in similar positions and ask them to see if the people on their list might be available for an interview. Because this is a formal program, our employees usually tell their friends that they are on their list and they hope that someday they will work at Severson. We've had very good success with this system, since we hire people who usually rate fairly high with the Five Cs. It's been especially effective in our production areas. Admittedly, it's more difficult at the senior management levels, but still effective. In fact, you were on our Sales Manager's list for quite some time. When the need materialized, we gave you a call and set up that fateful lunch. If you think about it, we could easily double the size of our company with little difficulty if we called everyone on every employee's list. It can get pretty tough to find good employees, but this system works.

"So Todd, I want you to do three things as a result of today's

233

meeting. First, you need to think about your junior. Which team member will you choose that makes the most sense, that you can support and defend in the position, and that will do a great job when you're gone? Second, I want you to pick an account-ability partner. I would suggest one of your peers who is another regional manager. One last comment on that. Don't pick a wom-an. We don't like to team up people of the opposite sex as ac-countability partners because we don't want to create a scenario for two people to become more than teammates. Third, I want you to make a list of two or three people who you would love to have working here."

Todd instantly thought about both Brian and Grant. Grant could do the same job he was doing and Brian could work some-where in the plant. That was an obvious choice for him.

As Blake walked Todd out of his office that week, he encour-aged him once again to take what he learned home and explain it to his family. Blake never told him this, but one of the reasons he had Todd explain it to his family was it was a method for him to remember what they had discussed. Once Todd got into the pattern of downloading what he had learned to his family, he kept better notes and formulated the best way to pass it on. It was information that Blake knew his family would benefit from, and it was one more tool to keep Todd engaged with his wife and kids. He was helping Todd enjoy the most important people in his life—his family.

## QUARTERLY SCORECARDS

The following week, Todd entered Blake's office for their last for-mal training session of the program. As Todd walked to his chair, he had a great sense that he had really accomplished something of value. He had that strong sense of enjoyment that comes with

COMPANYWIDE DEPLOYMENT OF THE PROGRAM

completing something big. The program he had learned was huge. There was just one more piece and he would be done...or so he thought.

Blake asked Todd to come over to his desk instead of meeting around the conference table where they normally met.

"Today we're going to go over our measurement system. In addition to our weekly assessment and scoring system, we do formal quarterly scorecards. I call it 360 degree scoring because we score each other from four different directions. We know that to make sure someone is really adhering to the program, they should be getting good scores from everyone around them. This includes their supervisor, their teammates, their customers or vendors and their subordinates. We know that if someone is scoring high in a few areas but low in others they are usually getting ahead at the expense of those areas they are scoring lower in. To put it another way, they are doing well at cultivating the orchards they are scoring high in but letting the other ones wither and die. Obviously the scoring system is designed for use in all aspects of our lives, not just at work. If you are using the program in all areas of your life, you should be able to score all areas of your life. Here at Severson, we've put our scoring system online and encouraged employees to obtain scores from people in their personal lives.

"Now let me explain how the scoring system works. It's a very objective system. The scorecard has 20 questions worth five points each for a total of 100 points. For each question, there are five possible answers, the best worth five points and the worst being 1 point. We wanted the tests to be objective so both the person being scored and the person scoring would both know exactly why they gave that particular score. We wanted scores to add up to 100 so it would be really easy for people to know whether they were performing at the A level, a score from 90 to 100; the B level, a score from 80 to 89; the C level, a score from 70 to 79; or at the D level or perhaps failing—a score of less than 70. We believe that for someone to be doing well they should be scoring 80% or better on all four scorecards. You'll remember we strive for 80% or better on our weekly scoring.

"I've printed out the scorecard for you to take a look at. Take it home and study it. If you feel up to it, make a number of copies and have your wife and kids score you. It's designed so that anyone in any direction can provide you with a score. Think about how people around you at work would score you, your customers, the people who report to you, your peers and how your boss would score you. If you keep a mental track of how they might score you, you may try to improve in that area before they do the real scoring."

Blake walked Todd to the door and said they would meet the following week.

**SEVERSON SYSTEMS**                                                      SCORECARD

**HONESTY AND INTEGRITY**
5=The most honest person I know
4=In the top 5 honest people I know
3=About the same as anyone else- relative honesty
2=Less honest than most
1=Watch out for this person

**DEPENDABLE AND RESPONSIVE**
5=100% dependable and responsive
4=80% dependable and responsive
3=60% dependable and responsive
2=50% dependable and responsive
1=Has no idea what dependability is

**FRIENDLY AND CARING**
5=Could regularly invite to dinner and enjoy it
4=Dinner once in a while would be okay
3=Could have dinner if I had to
2=Not sure I could make it through dinner
1=Can't see spending any time with this person

**RESPECTFUL AND POLITE**
5=High respect for all people
4=Good respect for all people
3=Respectful of some but not others
2=Little respect for anyone
1=No respect for anyone

**RESPECTFUL OF OTHER'S TIME**
5=Is never late
4=Late only once in a while
3=Late more than once month.
2=Is late on a regular basis
1=Is always late

**LISTENING SKILLS**
5=One of the best listeners I know
4=Usually hears what I'm saying
3=Sometimes hears what I'm saying
2=Seldom hears what I'm saying
1=Doesn't listen well at all

## COMMUNICATION SKILLS
5=Excellent communication and explanations
4=Good communications and explanations
3=Fair communications and explanations
2=Poor communications and explanations
1=No communication, no explanations

## IS A GOOD ROLE MODEL
5=I can only hope to be more like this person
4=I like 90% of what this person is all about
3=Not necessarily a good or bad role model
2=Clearly not a good role model
1=Nobody should model this person

## IS A GOOD COACH WHEN NECESSARY
5=Always brings out the best in me
4=Usually brings out the best in me
3=Sometimes brings out the best in me
2=Seldom brings out the best in me
1=Brings out the worst in me

## SENSITIVE TO OTHERS NEEDS
5=Highly sensitive
4=Very sensitive
3=Somewhat sensitive
2=Not very sensitive
1=Doesn't know what sensitivity is

## UNDERSTANDS HIS/HER ROLES
5=100% defined and followed
4=Usually defined and followed
3=Sometimes defined and followed
2=Defined often but not followed
1=My job is not defined

## IS ACCOUNTABLE
5=Takes feedback better than anyone
4=Takes feedback better than most
3=Takes feedback about like anyone
2=Doesn't take feedback well
1=Bites your head off when attempted

## SETS GOALS
5=Written annual, monthly, weekly, daily goals
4=Written goals of some timeframes
3=Some written goals
2=Has goals in his/her head
1=Doesn't know what goals are

## CLEARLY DEFINES EXPECTATIONS
5=Clearly defines and meets expectations
4=Usually defines and meets expectations
3=Sometimes defines and meets expectations
2=Almost never defines expectations
1=Doesn't know how to define expectations

## PRIORITIZES TASKS
5=Sets daily priority tasks
4=Sets weekly priority tasks
3=Sometimes sets priority tasks
2=Seldom prioritizes tasks
1=What's a priority?

## PROVIDES WEIGHTS TO PRIORITY LISTS
5=Defines the weight of every task
4=Defines the weight of most tasks
3=Sometimes defines the weights of tasks
2=Doesn't define the weight of tasks often
1=Doesn't know what a weight is

## ALIGNS EXPECTATIONS BOTH WAYS
5=Always aligns expectations using the Filter
4=Often aligns expectations using the Filter
3=Sometimes aligns expectations using the Filter
2=Sometimes aligns but not with the Filter
1=Has never seen the Filter

## DEMONSTRATES ETHICS AND VALUES
5=Highest level of ethical behavior I've seen
4=Very high levels of ethical behavior
3=Has good ethical behavior
2=Slightly lower than most on ethics
1=Watch out for this person

## ATTITUDE
5=Demonstrates 90% positive attitude
4=Usually demonstrates a positive attitude
3=Sometimes demonstrates a positive attitude
2=The cup is always half empty
1=Horrible attitude

## ENGAGES DEEPLY
5=One of the best people to talk to
4=Great person to talk to
3=Could take it or leave it
2=Not very engaging
1=I'd rather talk to my dog or cat

**Total your circled scores and write here:**

90–100% .... A— Excellent Score
80–89%...... B— Good Score
70–79%...... C— Fair Score
60–69%...... D— Poor Score
59% or less ... F— Failing Score

**CHAPTER SUMMARY**

- The program must be adopted and embraced by the person at the top.
  - Wherever the program begins.
  - The program can be forced one level up.
- Whoever is at the top spot teaches it to his/her direct reports.
  - They in turn teach it to those who report to them.
- Most companies and individuals fall short of their goals because they don't have anything that helps them deploy their plan throughout the year.
  - The *Right Side of the Equation* Program Calendar provides the discipline a company needs to achieve their goals.
- Everyone in the company should have an understudy. We call it your Junior.
  - Someone who has been trained to do the other's job in the event they are on vacation, sick or even die.
- The Junior Program improves productivity.
  - Employees and systems will improve as one person trains another.
  - It is the answer for the company to go on during any season.
  - Job description, accomplishments and the Filter can be used as the training curriculum.

- Everyone needs accountability. We recommend implementing an Accountability Partner Program—at all levels, especially the CEO level.
- If you like your employees, you would probably like their friends. Their friends too would make good employees—the Best Friend Program.
- The Best Friend Program asks every employee to make a list of their friends they would like to see come and work with them.
- The Best Friend Program allows you to double the size of your company very quickly.
- Throughout school, you are given quarterly report cards. The quarterly Scorecards are similar.

**Points to Ponder**

- Will you teach the *Right Side of the Equation* Program to those who report to you?
- Will you follow the plan by implementing the Annual Calendar?
- Do you have a Junior?
    - — Is he or she capable of doing your job?
- Do you have an Accountability Partner?
- Which of your friends would you like to see come and work with you?
- Do you have a quarterly scoring system?

# 19

# Graduation

I T HAD BEEN SEVERAL WEEKS since Todd started with Severson. He implemented each of the prior week's sessions with his team and with his family. He had even brought Grant up to speed on most of what he had learned. Todd's life had changed dramatically. He now understood why he had joined Severson Systems and what was different about them.

For the first time in his life, Todd was focusing on the things that mattered most—his family and friends first, and then the people he worked with. He was working with a deliberate purpose and plan. He had goals at home and at the office. He was setting weekly objectives with expectations. He was holding 50/50 Meetings with the individuals on his team and with his wife and kids. He was in a supportive environment for the first time in his life. He had never known what that looked like before. And he was more interested in what was happening with the people at work, at home and with his friends than he was his golf clubs, his motorcycle and any of his other possessions. Those things didn't mean as much to him anymore. For the first time in years he understood the relationship he needed to have with his kids and he was making it happen. And for the first time in many years, he and his wife were focusing on each other's needs and enjoying each other. He honestly loved his wife more now than he could ever remember.

Blake hadn't told Todd anything he hadn't heard before. He had heard everything he learned from Blake in bits and pieces throughout his life. What made it different was the way it was packaged. It was a specific program that incorporated all of these important components into one easily defined and easily followed plan.

Todd dropped by Blake's office at the normal time that next week. He wanted to tell Blake that it felt strange not to meet with him. Blake had changed his life in just a series of short meetings. He clearly felt more joy and happiness because he was focusing on the things that mattered most in life. In addition, he was working in a place that recognized this and modeled it. Blake told Todd that afternoon that the process hasn't ended, rather had just begun. Blake showed Todd a new way to play the game of life. Now it was up to Todd to live it. As they talked about the program, Blake gave Todd yet another piece of advice about the *Right Side of the Equation.*

"Todd, the program you've learned can be taught to anyone. It's not just for you and me; it's for everyone. Relational Intelligence teaches people how to fulfill their primary needs in life. I encourage you to tell your friends about it and other people you meet. Practice it daily and you can live a fulfilled life with purpose."

That comment made Todd think back to the three most important things in his life. At that moment he remembered Blake had a different number one item on his list. It was his faith. Todd asked Blake, "You told me you would tell me about the number one item on your list sometime. I'd like to hear about that."

Maybe there was something to it that Todd needed to hear about. After all, it seemed to be a big part of Blake's life.

"I'd be happy to tell you about the role that my faith plays in my life. Why don't we set up a few weekly meetings on Friday afternoons?"

**CHAPTER SUMMARY**

- The *Right Side of the Equation* has components you've been aware of all your life.

  — It is packaged in a way that allows you to focus on the most important things.

- Setting goals is important.

- Goals won't materialize without the involvement of people.

- Pursuing, pleasing and meeting the needs of people will bring the best results.

- Focus on the things that matter most in life.

## POINTS TO PONDER

- There are three steps to the Program:

  1  Set goals.

  2  Determine who will accomplish
     what by when.

  3  Deploy the program weekly using
     the 50/50 Meeting and the rules.

- Will you seek to pursue, please and meet
  the needs of all the people around you?

- Focus on the three things that
  matter most in your life.

# 20

# Mastering
# Relational Intelligence

R EAD A BOOK ON FLYING and you'll learn the rules, methods, language, and the physics of flying. You may completely understand every aspect of how a plane flies. You
may even be able to get a plane off the ground and land it. But
you won't master flying until you gain the experience by logging
in many hours of practice with someone coaching you through
the process.

The same is true of Relational Intelligence. Mastering Relational Intelligence will not happen the instant you complete this
book. I have provided steps, tools and processes you can use, but
now you must practice it. The good news is when you begin to
practice it, there's an immediate payoff. You will fulfill at least one
of the top three most important needs in your life—a need for
relationship.

Do you want better relationships with those you love? Do
you want to enjoy your work environment? Would you like contentment in your career, knowing you're achieving your goals
through great relationships? These are rhetorical questions. Focus
on the *Right Side of the Equation* and your answers to these questions will materialize.

There's one other significant thing we've learned by deploy-

THE RIGHT SIDE OF THE EQUATION

ing the *Right Side of the Equation*. The right side actually validates the left side. When we work as a team with our employees, they help determine if our goals and objectives are realistic, reasonable and achievable. Our goals and objectives are driven by the relationships we nurture. Building consensus from everyone involved before tackling the year has been very beneficial for many companies.

Here's a recap of the program:

1. Get your head in the game! (The *Right Side of the Equation*)

2. Write down your goals. (Step One)

   a. For your faith

   b. For yourself

   c. For your marriage

   d. For your family

   e. For your job

   f. And for the other five orchards in your life (p. 198)

3. Consider who is necessary to complete these goals. (Step Two)

   a. The right person in the right seat—The Five Cs.

   b. They accomplish goals by a certain date.

4. Seek to pursue, please and meet the needs of those around you. (Step Three)

5. Learn how to conduct a 50/50 Meeting.

   a. First communicate how they can be successful.

   b. Then, spend an equal amount of time talking about the orchards of life.

6. Set and live by absolute rules.

Blake Severson learned to master Relational Intelligence and became extremely successful in the process. He focused on the things that mattered most to him and to others—the people. It was difficult because he wasn't naturally a relational person. He struggles. But it's a worthwhile struggle with measurable results, like exercising at the gym.

His original intentions for the development of the program were to fulfill his goals. He thought these goals were to have a successful business and make money. He learned in the process the real payoff is to enjoy the people around him and vice versa. Having a successful business means nothing if he can't share that success with loved ones. Todd Hanson agrees.